# PRAISE FOR NICOLAS ROTHWELL'S *BELOMOR*

'I found myself completely captured by the lucid detachment and uncanny atmosphere of Nicolas Rothwell's *Belomor*, four narratives that range from exquisitely shaped nuggets of art history to suggestive character studies of eccentrics and esoteric quests, and from European cities in the midst of destruction to the hidden world of the Australian bush…You feel as if imbibing too much at once might be awfully dangerous.'
*Times Literary Supplement*, Best Books 2013

'[A] meditative journey through the empty ruins of the world, Nicolas Rothwell's *Belomor* is by turns ravishing and dismaying, a novel which is also an essay on art and a chantepleure on meaning and impermanence.'
*Australian Book Review*, Best Books 2013

'Beautiful and mesmerising…Engages the intellect as well as the emotions.' *Australian*

'This is a remarkable work, tinged with sadness and verging on poetry, tempered now and then with humour and authentic historical insight. It is a contemporary Australian novel of such beauty, it's hard to find a precedent.' *Age*

'Bewitching…A hymn of praise to the north and its inhabitants.' *Herald Sun*

'Rothwell's considerable achievement is to provoke an emotional response to [his protagonists'] philosophising. His gorgeous and fluid prose produces a sort of on-the-page hymn to life and death.' *Advertiser*

'Melancholy, singular, exhilarating, *Belomor* reads like a haunted history of the world.' Delia Falconer

# QUICKSILVER

# Nicolas Rothwell

# Quicksilver

TEXT PUBLISHING
MELBOURNE AUSTRALIA

textpublishing.com.au

The Text Publishing Company
Swann House
22 William Street
Melbourne Victoria 3000
Australia

Abridged earlier versions of parts of this book appeared in *The Best Australian
Essays 2012*, the *Monthly*, *Meanjin* and the *Australian*.

First published in 2016 by The Text Publishing Company

Design by W. H. Chong
Typeset by J & M Typesetting

Printed in Australia by Griffin Press, an Accredited ISO AS/NZS 14001:2004
Environmental Management System printer.

National Library of Australia Cataloguing-in-Publication entry
ISBN:    9781925355574 (hardback)
ISBN:    9781925410006 (ebook)
Creator: Rothwell, Nicolas, author.
Title:    Quicksilver / by Nicolas Rothwell.
Dewey Number: 919.41

*In memory of Nyurapayia Nampitjinpa*

# CONTENTS

*'Be not wise in thine own eyes'*

# I

# Into the Red

It was the cold, dry midwinter season in the desert, when frost falls on the claypans; the skies are clear, and set the mind to roam. I began my days of journeying: I drove west from Papunya to Kintore and Kiwirrkurra, to Well 33 and on, past red dunes and salt lakes, past the ramparts of the Telfer goldmine, until the ranges of the Pilbara drew near, and I was almost within reach of my initial destination, Marble Bar. All through that crossing the country was quiet; the horizons were a transparent blue. There had been fires: the sandhill crests were bare. Bush turkeys stalked through the remnant spinifex, stretching out their necks and gazing fixedly towards the sun. The roads were empty: for the best part of a week I saw no trace of man and his works. It was a spectacle of solitude—much like the landscape described by the first European explorer to make a successful transit of that country, the gloomy Colonel Warburton, whose uncommunicative eyes stare out from the frontispiece of his *Journey Across the Western Interior of Australia*, published in London in 1875.

Although Warburton and his men were the first outsiders to see the blood-red mesas and the open dune fields west of Lake Gregory, in his account of his expedition he pays scant attention to the features of the desert, concentrating instead on the privations his party endured in the course of their ten-month passage, as they laboured over the sandhills, slaughtering and devouring their pack camels one by one. By the last stage of the journey Warburton was full of anguish:

> Night-work, tropical heat, no sleep, poor food and very limited allowance of water are, when combined, enough to reduce any man's strength; it is no wonder then that I can scarcely crawl. What a country! Did any men before traverse such a tract of desert? I think not.

In the end he fell so ill he could no longer sit in his saddle. He had to be tied full-length on the animal's back, and so, trussed up like a piece of baggage, he proceeded until the dunes gave way to a range on the horizon, and then a rocky creek bed came into view. It led in turn to a wide sandy channel, lined by tall gumtrees—the Oakover, the great inland river of the northwest. The men made camp. They were within reach of safety. 'This must be a noble river,' mused Warburton, 'when the floods come down. The bed is wide and gravelly, fringed with magnificent cajeput or paper-bark trees. How grateful is its lovely and shady refuge from the burning sun after the frightful sand-hills in which we have been so long baked.' The expedition's diet improved: a teal, small bush pheasants, a fish, a shag. 'Occasionally an iguana or cockatoo enlivens our fare.'

Warburton moved his men to high ground. There were strong winds blowing round them, and heavy clouds went scudding across the sky. The weather cleared. The last camel was killed, skinned and cut up. That night his wish came true; the landscape showed them its other face:

> To our great surprise we were awakened at 3 a.m. by the roaring of running water. The river was down, running with a current of about three knots an hour. In the evening there was not a drop of water in the river—in the morning a stream 300 yards wide was sweeping down with timber and ducks floating on it. The sight was most beautiful at sunrise.

Such, still, is the Oakover: relief after unending desert, the first gleaming flash of blue after the dunes and spinifex, tall fringing gumtrees, deep rock pools, curved, high embankments of river sand. I stopped. I got out of the four-wheel-drive and walked—along the channel, up a side creek. It wound towards the hills. Its slopes steepened; it became a gorge line: a ravine. The sun was beating down; and at that moment I became aware of another presence, breathing, watchful, close at hand. There, right in front of me, was a large perentie lizard, unmoving, its forefeet stretched out in front of its body, its head held slightly up from the rock. Doubtless, I said to myself, a lineal descendant of one of the 'iguanas' that had eased Colonel Warburton's recovery in this same stretch of landscape all those years ago. The creature gazed at me in solemn fashion, and made no attempt to move. Its forked tongue flicked out and back. Should I show any sign of having seen it? Should I make a gesture or a sound?

My thoughts flew at once to the most famous lizard anecdote in world literature: the tale of Leo Tolstoy's meeting with a rather smaller species of lizard, a Black Sea gecko, which he encountered in Yalta, while walking along the road that leads up to the ornate Dulber Palace, a crenellated pleasure dome, built by Grand Duke Pyotr Nikolaevich just two decades before the revolution came. Maxim Gorky, the prince of proletarian writers, who revered Tolstoy as his exemplar in both art and life, describes the episode in the reminiscences he sketched out in his years of exile, marooned on Cape Sorrento—and perhaps it was the rhyme between the Mediterranean and the Crimean coastal landscapes that kept the incident so vivid in his thoughts. He narrates it in his most clipped and thrown-off style:

> Leo Tolstoy once asked a lizard in a low voice: 'Are you happy, eh?' The lizard was sunning itself on a rock in the bushes along the road, and Tolstoy stood facing it with his hands stuck into his leather belt. And looking around carefully, that great man confessed to the lizard: 'I'm not...'

The truth, the depth of the heart, presented to a living thing that cannot understand or make reply. Does the world of nature hear us, or see or heed what lies within us—or does it merely set a frame around us, a strange, distant frame that draws all our secrets out? I stared back at the perentie, and saw the lovely sand-shaded lozenge pattern on its skin, and its long, thin tail, and the dark pupils of its eyes—and doubtless such questions were somewhere in me—but now I call the moment back, I realise that the poor animal was simply too cold to move. It was sunning itself at the peak of the day's heat. It was in the midst of its time of hibernation; it was weak from hunger, and clinging to the edge of life.

I went back along the riverbed. Soon I would drive on,

through the ranges, until the track ran into a sealed mining road, and dust trails from far-off road trains appeared. I was at the desert's frontier, the point where the world of stillness and silences gives way to mankind's order: disruptions, transformations, reverberating sound. In the former, the mind is prone to nameless fears; it starts at shadows; it hears murmurs and voices carrying on the wind. In the latter, where lines and sharp angles hold sway, the self is pinioned by external forces; it is unable to sense its own shape; a quite different species of horror presses down. What lies beyond the borders of what we can know? What awaits us, and stands on the other side of our every look and glance?

It seems next to impossible to make prolonged trips into the desert and the rangelands without being afflicted by such questions. They rise up even as one seeks to set them at rest; they redouble; they fill the void. No wonder all man's spiritual endeavours are devoted to vanquishing the constant parade within us of speculation and surmise, for the world that exceeds us makes plain the limits to our mastery, and makes plain that we are not gods on earth—that we must, like all that is made of matter, pass away.

*

These fears particularly tormented Tolstoy, that most serene and Apollonian-seeming of novelists, a writer who soared on the wings of narrative, who felt no bounds constraining his craft, who allowed himself to think and feel his way into the minds and hearts of great princes and humble servants, and even devoted a section of *Anna Karenina* to the beliefs and hopes of Laska, Levin's favourite hunting dog. They also troubled Gorky, whose reminiscences of Tolstoy are a kind of distorted presentation of his own ideas about the writer's task in the modern world.

Their conversations took place in the Crimea over a period of five months, beginning in November 1901. Gorky had just been released from jail, thanks in great part to Tolstoy's intercession. He stayed at the health resort of Oleiz, close to Gaspra, the estate of Countess Panina, where Tolstoy was himself recuperating from prolonged illness. This was the only extended time the two men spent together. Tolstoy was at the end of his prodigious career in literature. Gorky's was just beginning. They entertained a fascination for each other, despite the deep differences between them in matters of religion and politics.

When Gorky received the news of Tolstoy's death, he set his feelings down: 'It is a blow to the heart; I have howled out my grief and injury, and now, in a half-crazed state, I picture him as I have seen and known him, and feel an agonising need to speak of him.' Gorky went on to describe an occasion when he had come upon Tolstoy sitting alone among the rocks on the Gaspra shore, gazing far out to sea. The forces of the sky and wind and sun seemed to whirl round that ancient, silver-bearded figure, lost in thought. How magical he looked, how like a prophet. Gorky felt himself filled with both rapture and horror.

> There is much in Lev Nikolayevich that at times has evoked something close to hatred in me, much that has been like an oppressive burden on my soul. He had risen too high above the human world, and gone off into some wilderness where, concentrating all the powers of his spirit to the utmost, he gazes in solitude at the main thing, death.

And this anguish in the face of death's presence in our midst loomed large for Gorky, too. Tolstoy's fear of death exactly mirrored fears that lurked in him: and at the heart of everything, at the climax of his portrait, he placed the 'Arzamas horror', a hinge point in Tolstoy's life.

It was August 1869. The manuscript of *War and Peace* had just been completed. Tolstoy was on his way to inspect an estate in Penza province, far to the east of Moscow. The journey was long, with many stops, and he chanced to spend one night at a hotel in the town of Arzamas. He lay awake. As he wrote to his wife, Sofia Andreyevna, 'I wanted to get some sleep, but suddenly I was seized by angst, fear and horror the likes of which I have never encountered before:

God forbid that anyone ever has to suffer the torment that gripped me so severely.'

A full fifteen years later Tolstoy tried to record this episode in more detail in a short story that he never succeeded in finishing, 'Notes of a Madman'. The central character is travelling on the same route to Penza, and stops with his manservant, Andrei, at a hotel in Arzamas. He lies awake. His mind races: 'Why did I come here, where am I going? Why and what am I running away from? I am running away from something horrible, but I cannot do so. I am always with myself, always torturing myself.' He goes out into the corridor, and sees Andrei and the nightwatchman, both fast asleep. He had wanted to flee what was tormenting him in the room, but it came out after him; it darkened everything around him. What was he afraid of? 'You are afraid of me,' the voice of death answers him, inaudibly: 'I am here.' At this point his despair multiplies. He is alive, but death is there before him; death is all about him. He lives, and is dying: there is a dreadful inner conflict. Almost to save himself he snatches up a copper candlestick with a burnt-out red wax candle, and lights it—he stares into the red, stares deeply into it, as if it might reveal some secret to him, but the red light coming from it keeps saying the same thing: 'There is nothing in life but death, and it should not be there.'

\*

Death tested Maxim Gorky often. It confronted him repeatedly, it claimed those closest to him, it ambushed him in many guises; and when he in his turn had become the most famous Russian writer of his age, the circumstances of his own death and the controversies that swirled around it long outlived him. Years after the revolution, years after his attempt to describe Tolstoy's horror in Arzamas, he was enticed back to the Soviet Union for an official visit, ostensibly to celebrate his sixtieth birthday. His days of independence now came to an end. He made his peace with Bolshevism. Soon he became the regime's most favoured literary celebrity: a symbol of the cause. His cult grew. He was given an art-nouveau mansion in Moscow to serve as his home, a dacha outside the capital and an estate of his own in the Crimea. The city where he was born, Nizhny Novgorod, was rebaptised with his name: it was known as Gorky all through the ensuing decades of communism.

In 1929 he embarked on a triumphal journey across the Soviet hinterland, escorted by a large deputation of secret police. He was keen to inspect the penal institutions of the workers' state, given his strong interest in the principle of reform through labour, and his own youthful experience of the lower depths—and it was only natural for him to make an inspection visit to the jewel of the Soviet prison system, the camp archipelago of Solovetsky in the White Sea. On

20 June, the steamer *Gleb Boyki* arrived at the landing stage on the Bay of Prosperity, just beneath the Solovki Kremlin, with Gorky and his entourage on board. There he was, tall, instantly recognisable. He had a heavy moustache. He wore a plain overcoat. On his head, pushed back at a rakish angle, in Lenin's style, was a workman's flat cap. The convict labourers watched with interest from their cell windows.

There are many accounts of Gorky's visit, and though they differ in their details its broad lines are clear enough. Everything had been carefully prepared in advance by the authorities. Fir trees from the taiga had been cut down and relocated along the road to make the camp seem more cheerful. Clean clothes were issued to the inmates; the hospital wards were spotless; the patients, all wearing brand-new dressing gowns, were lined up on both sides of the entrance and the stairs. Gorky looked in on one of the barracks. He spoke there, by his own request, alone, to a fourteen-year-old boy he singled out. He asked for details of the conditions in the camp. For forty minutes he stayed there, talking. When he came out, he was in tears, for all to see. Next it was the punishment cells, which had been cleaned up. The prisoners on show there had been given newspapers to read. Gorky went in, and went up to one of the readers, and quietly turned his newspaper the right way up. When there was a danger he might catch a glimpse of the shivering, half-naked labour battalions on the shore, the men were rounded up, pressed together and covered with a tarpaulin for as long as they remained in his field of view.

As soon as Gorky and his party had left, the punishments began. Those who had attempted to speak to him received extended sentences. The fourteen-year-old was taken away and killed. Some months afterwards, Gorky wrote a travel sketch, describing the prison islands and the camps. How beautiful the landscape was, how picturesque the old buildings. In the rooms that he inspected the softness and kindness of the regime was plain to see: 'four or six beds, each decorated with personal items, flowers on the windowsills'. Solovetsky was a new kind of camp, a 'school of labour', forging new worker-citizens for the Soviet state.

Some four years later the first great project undertaken by the workers of the archipelago was completed—the White Sea Canal, which cuts through the granite rock of Karelia, a waterway constructed by an army of one hundred thousand convicts at the cost of ten thousand lives. Even before the last locks and barrages were finished it became the focus of intense propaganda. A commemorative book was prepared under the editorial control of the secret police. Gorky was put in charge. A meeting took place at his home, with Stalin in attendance. It seemed logical to Gorky that a collective of thirty-six writers should be assembled, a standard work brigade, just like the brigades that worked on the new collective farms set up to build communism. Stalin was in agreement: writers were the 'engineers of human souls'.

Shortly after Stalin had made the inaugural steamer trip down the canal in August 1933, Gorky led a delegation of one hundred and twenty writers on a literary cruise; the photographer Rodchenko was on hand to record the journey. The book came out: it was titled *The Canal Named for Stalin*. Copies were distributed at the Seventeenth Congress of the Communist Party. The redemptive message was plain: 'In changing nature, man changes himself.' It was translated into many languages, and distributed around the world. But the logic of Stalin's state was inexorable. Gorky had become, as a result of his manufactured prominence, both a treasure and a threat. By the end of 1934 he was being kept in an informal detention in his Moscow mansion. Maxim Peshkov, his beloved son, died in mysterious circumstances. His own health deteriorated: he was gravely ill with tuberculosis.

In June 1936, Gorky's death from heart disease was announced. It was widely assumed that poison was the true cause. His brain was surgically removed within hours, and taken to the Neurological Institute in Moscow, where it remains still. His funeral was an extravaganza of choreographed mourning. Stalin was among the pallbearers who conveyed his body to its appointed tomb in the Kremlin Wall.

A few more years and Gorky's star was on the wane. By the time I began covering the Soviet Union and Eastern Europe as a correspondent in the 1980s, it was in eclipse. His novels were unread in the West, his volumes of reminiscences and memoirs quite forgotten. A scatter of official institutions, streets and factories still bore his name, though, as did the river town of Gorky, which was a destination of the greatest interest to foreign journalists in those years. It had been chosen by the authorities as the place of internal exile for the nuclear physicist and human-rights campaigner Andrei Sakharov.

What schemes and subterfuges did we not resort to in our attempts to gain permits for travel there from the International Correspondents Assistance and Friendship Bureau! How artfully I framed my proposals and requests: an investigation of the baroque Stroganov churches and the old citadel, a visit to the University of Linguistics, a dispatch on the childhood of the composer Balakirev—all were turned down with unconcealed contempt. Instead we received detailed briefings on Sakharov and his latest libels against the Soviet system. We were lectured on the wellsprings of the dissident movement and its covert plans to subvert socialism. We were watched, and shadowed, and chaperoned by helpful minders from the Novosti press agency on every road trip we made beyond the outer Moscow ring. All this in a bid to keep the words of Academician Sakharov from reaching the outside world.

His banishment had been enacted on 22 January 1980, in dramatic style. It was Sakharov's habit, every Tuesday, to attend a seminar at the Physics Institute of the Academy of Science. He ordered a car, as usual, from the academy's motor pool, and set out. The police blocked the road and intercepted him. He was escorted to the prosecutor's office on Pushkin Street, and there informed of his fate. That same afternoon he was taken, together with his wife, Yelena Bonner, to Domodedovo Airport and bundled onto a special plane supplied with a doctor and gourmet food.

The minutes of the Politburo meeting of 3 January that formalised this decision have an unusual verve. Yuri Andropov, who was at the time the chairman of the KGB, took the lead. Andropov was at the vanguard of the regime's latest crackdown on antisocial elements. He had already ordered the arrest of all known members of human-rights organisations in Moscow and Kiev; his troops had raided the offices of Samizdat journals; he was in the midst of a campaign against Christian activists. 'Sakharov is the initiator of all the anti-Soviet undertakings,' said Andropov at the outset. To which the foreign minister, Andrei Gromyko, replied: 'The question of Sakharov has ceased to be a purely domestic question. He finds an enormous number of responses abroad.

All the anti-Soviet scum, all this rabble revolves around Sakharov. It is impossible to ignore the situation any longer.' The solution was obvious: away with him—into exile, to the closed city that preserved the proletarian writer's name.

Sakharov was a man of high cultural formation, and of great gifts which were already manifest in early childhood. He had a special aptitude for physics. Soon after his graduate training he began to publish scientific papers of promise; then, in 1949, he seemed to vanish from the world. He had been drafted into the Soviet nuclear program, and sent to the secret facility of Arzamas-16: the Installation, as Sakharov calls it in his memoir. It had been built by convict labourers. They were still at work when Sakharov arrived: 'Every morning long grey lines of men in quilted jackets, guard dogs at their heels, passed by our curtained windows.' Soon he was assigned to a special group investigating the possibility of building a hydrogen bomb. The milieu had its effect on him: 'We were encouraged to throw ourselves into our work by the fierce concentration of a single goal, and perhaps also by the proximity of the labour camp and strict regimentation. The rest of the world was far away, somewhere beyond two barbed-wire fences.'

Three years later the Soviet Union successfully detonated its first thermonuclear device. Sakharov was regarded as responsible for the design. Suddenly he was the master, the hero of the state. Everything appeared possible for him in those days. The nuclear age had dawned—but with it came repeated atmospheric testing by both superpowers, and the certainty of large-scale casualties as a result of radiation fallout. Sakharov felt an anguished foreboding, a sense of complicity. He pleaded for an end to tests in the atmosphere: his pleas were brushed away. This was the moment when the choice that would define him loomed.

> I could not stop something I knew was wrong and unnecessary. I had an awful sense of powerlessness. After that I was a different man. I broke with my surroundings. It was a basic break. The atomic question was always half science, half politics. After that first break, everything was natural.

He separated himself decisively from the political establishment. He resolved 'to speak out, to put everything else aside'. In 1968, a year of deep crisis for the Soviet system, he succeeded in publishing 'Progress, Co-existence and Intellectual Freedom', a landmark plea for demilitarisation and democratic reform. It was printed in a Dutch newspaper, but its first readers were the KGB, who had been thoughtfully passed a copy by the secretary Sakharov had asked to type up the manuscript.

From that day until his removal from Moscow he was the central figure of the unofficial opposition movement. The decision to send him into exile merely increased his prominence. All through his six years in Gorky he lived under tight police observation, virtually confined to a modest apartment in a tower block. During that time he resumed work on his memoirs. He tried always to keep the manuscript with him, but the KGB went to great lengths to steal it, once purloining Sakharov's bag from a dentist's waiting room; once smashing his car window, drugging him and removing the satchel with the handwritten pages from the floor behind the driver's seat.

Ordeals of this kind formed the texture of Sakharov's time in Gorky, which came to an abrupt end soon after the election of the reformist Mikhail Gorbachev as the party chief. Sakharov was now invited to return home. For three years he was able to play a part in his country's political debates. He was elected to the Congress of People's Deputies in the spring of 1989, and died that December, just as the revolutionary upheavals in Central Europe were dismantling the client regimes of Soviet communism.

*

It was not until long afterwards that I was able to fulfil my plan of those days, and make a trip by car from Moscow eastwards, to the old provincial centres of the Volga: to

Yaroslavl, and Kazan, and Astrakhan, and above all to the place that once bore Gorky's name, Nizhny Novgorod. I wanted to see the city in dual perspective: to see its present guise, but also recognise its past, the features of its streets that dated from Soviet times, when it was a showcase of the regime, and its factories and railway bridges were the pride of the state—and I thought I might be helped in this task by a visit to the little apartment in the Scherbinki district, where Sakharov had been required to live. It was a museum now, but somehow nothing of Sakharov's presence seemed to survive in its well-kept and silent rooms.

I made dutiful inspection tours of the various churches, shrines and galleries I had wished to see so long ago, but it was not until I had found a quiet space in the park beneath the red walls of the Kremlin that I felt some kind of peace and space for reflection descend. It was a soft spring day. The light was clear. High above me the contrails of jetliners were visible in the blue of the sky. I took out an old copy of Sakharov's memoirs, a book that has always been a work of majesty for me, a work at once precise in its description of a single life's experiences and soaring in its view of man's responsibilities in the world. I remembered the strong sense I had when reading it on its first appearance, shortly after Sakharov's death, that the tone of his personality had lingered in its pages: that his willingness to see a purpose in his life beyond the satisfactions of individual fulfilment had been enough to preserve, for a while, the aura of his character on Earth, so much so that he seemed to be murmuring the words of his book softly into his reader's ear; one could feel the inflections in his sentences and the lilted intonation in the clusters of his words. I opened it, and found one of its central passages, in which Sakharov seeks to capture something of his thoughts on the relationship between science and the hazy world of faith:

> Today, deep in my heart, I do not know where I stand on religion. I don't believe in any dogma and I dislike official churches, especially those closely tied to the state, those of a predominantly ceremonial character, or those tainted by fanaticism and intolerance. And yet I am unable to imagine the universe and human life without some guiding principle, without a source of spiritual warmth that is non-material and not bound by physical laws.

I set the book aside, and let those words fall through me, and looked round, at the parkland, at the linden trees in flower, the hawthorns, the oaks and tall, spreading chestnuts, the light on their leaves, their warmth—the same warmth and light that shines on the bank of the Oakover, at the desert's edge, where the kites soar and perenties bask, amid the bloodwoods and the river gums, the rocks, the sand and spinifex.

# II

# Quicksilver

*Reflections*

In my childhood, now so distant from me that the precious sights I saw then take on the hazy contours of a dream, I went often with my family to a resort in the High Tatra Mountains of Slovakia, Tatranská Lomnica, and stayed for months on end, throughout high summer, in the rundown fastness of the Praha Hotel. The Praha, in those last years of the Czechoslovak People's Republic, was an institution struggling against its own identity. It was an elaborate creation: gabled façades, grand balconies, high-ceilinged ballrooms lit by chandeliers. It had been built at the close of the nineteenth century, when the region was still under Habsburg rule, and the spa towns of north Slovakia were the chosen destination of a select coterie: bankers, opera singers, tycoons and provincial landowners from all across that corner of the fading empire. But with the change in regime had come a change of guests. Now those long, dark-carpeted corridors were trudged down by regional communist party secretaries, factory representatives from the valleys of East Slovakia and favoured members of the national ice-hockey team. The portrait of Emperor Franz Josef above the fireplace in the smoking lounge had been replaced by a blurry, impressionistic rendition of Karl Marx at his work desk, pensive, pen in hand, sporting a red bow tie, the forces of the dialectic wheeling inside his head. Outside the buildings, there had been little progress in the construction of socialism. High above the hotel, beyond pine-covered spurs and valleys, rose the mountains. Their dark stone blades reached up into a deep blue sky. Their lower slopes were covered by a fretwork of regimented, well-kept walking trails.

How often I picture in my memory those winding paths, and the peaks above—and, far up the flank of the highest mountain, the observatory at Skalnaté Pleso, its twin domes gleaming in the sun. It was there, in mid-1939, that the astronomer Antonín Bečvář set up a high-altitude scientific station, and began his long-term program of cometary research. Nothing, in those years, was free from the touch of war and politics: the observatory had been born from the Munich Agreement, which obliged the Czechoslovak state to surrender its northeastern lands. But in this disaster lurked a rare opportunity. At Bečvář's urging, the large reflector telescope from Stara Dala in the frontier region was relocated to the High Tatras, where the atmosphere was thin and the seeing was ideal.

For some while, the astronomers worked there quietly, above the tree line, among the golden eagles and the chamois, quite removed from the Wagnerian struggles being played out in the world beneath them, close though those dramas and sufferings were—until May 1945, the very last days of wartime, when Bečvář, at the risk of his life, stood guard at the entrance to the observatory and warded off the retreating German army's demolition squads. He had only five more years, five years on the mountain, until the new communist regime dismissed him from his paradise, but that was long enough for him to complete the majestic sky charts that bear his name— Bečvář's *Atlas Coeli*.

Those sixteen maps, hand-drawn, were works of art as much as jewels of science. Nebulae and clusters, variables and double stars, the elusive outlines of the Milky Way and its dark, obscuring interstellar clouds—all are shown by Bečvář in the most subtle detail. The night sky comes alive; it is ordered in its beauty, made comprehensible. No star watcher who gazes into the *Atlas Coeli* fails to wonder at its maker's precision of eye or delicacy of hand. But Bečvář's gifts went far beyond his capacity to map the random scatter of the stars. He was a student of pattern, a seeker of form in nature.

He made another atlas, equally splendid, but much less well known, of the cloudscapes visible from his eyrie in the Tatras. He produced a book of austere photographic studies of the mountains. He even wrote, during the wartime years, a novel, *Last Summer*, which bears the strong impress of that languishingly romantic region, where so many nostalgia-laden books have been dreamed into life.

*

He left the mountains. His death came early, the result of a recurring bout of pneumonia, which he tried to resist by drastically increasing his workload. A detailed obituary was written by his great heir in the literary-accented tradition of Czech astrophysics, Zdeněk Kopal. It was on display in the little museum at the observatory, which one could visit after a short walk from the midway station of the funicular that ran to the Lomnický peak, and I remember seeing it there, behind glass, elegantly framed, and standing on tiptoe to read it, and being overwhelmed. How not to be struck by the character of the scientist sketched out in Kopal's words?

> He combined the true idealism of a dedicated soul with indefatigable zeal and modesty which endeared him to his friends, now greatly saddened by his passing, the circle of whom was never very wide owing to his shy and retiring nature—yet although he never travelled abroad

and was not personally known to many, the renown of his cartographic work spans the seven seas.

That last phrase seemed especially beautiful to me. I repeated it to myself. It stayed in my thoughts down the years; it would surface inside me like a token of the past's mysterious persistence—and perhaps it was this unusually precise memory from childhood that spurred me on, one weekend at the height of the upheavals of late 1989 in Central Europe, to make a trip from Bratislava to the mountains, and revisit the Praha Hotel.

*

Those were days when almost anything seemed possible: when foreign correspondents chasing from city to city had the sense of being plunged into an unending dream. Dictators fell, dissidents prevailed, agents of the state betrayed their masters, the structures of a generation gave way. Life itself seemed quite molten; the future was too lightning-bright to see. I remember feeling permanently lightheaded, and also watchful, fearful, on edge—and those were the colours of my thoughts that weekend morning as I took the main road north, early, my photographer half-asleep in the passenger seat alongside.

We passed a set of unmanned checkpoints. We overtook a slow-moving column of armoured cars. With me I had a little shortwave—I listened to it almost constantly during those months. I tuned it to the Radio Free Europe signal. I held it up against my ear to catch the news. Demonstrations in the central square of Sofia, in front of Aleksander Nevsky Cathedral; pleas for calm from the leaders of the protest movement. In Berlin, first talks between the leaders of East and West Germany after the opening of the Wall. Clashes in the Romanian border town of Timişoara, gunfire heard. And in Czechoslovakia, what? Chaos, vacuum, murk.

I drove at speed: through Trenčín, through Žilina. There, ahead, rising from the smoky, dirty swirl of cloud were the high peaks of the Tatras, shining white from early falls of snow. At which point the photographer, whom I had come to admire, both for his sangfroid and for his air of graceful reticence, turned to me.

'Take that road,' he said, 'please,' and so urgent was the tone in his voice that I complied, without a word, and we headed east, on a winding forest route. It followed the curves of a river channel. Another turn, and then another. He made a sign. We stopped. We were at the entrance to a ruined graveyard. The tombstones were tilted at odd angles; their surfaces were dark and damp. I walked through, still clutching the radio, making my way between the graves. The photographer was kneeling down beside a headstone: it was cracked. He traced out with his fingers the emblems carved onto it: the sun, the moon, even the planets—Saturn and its rings. The letters on the stone were Hebrew.

'My great-grandfather's tomb,' he said.

'He was an astronomer!'

'More a magician. More a man who studied the stars.'

'Strange,' I said, then, 'to find a Jewish graveyard, so far from any town.'

'It's not a Jewish cemetery,' said he. 'It's a Frankist one.'

I looked at him.

'You know that story?' he asked me. 'The story of the Frankist movement?'

'Vaguely,' I said.

'There's nothing vague about it'—and he began to tell the tale.

I settled back, and listened, leaning against the headstone—and though years have passed since then, I have never wholly broken free from that day, when empires were falling all about me, and I first gained a sense of what the darkness at the heart of religion could be.

*

Jacob Frank enters the historical record in the mid-eighteenth century. He emerges from Podolia, a frontier land on the southeastern fringe of Europe, with the river city of Vinnitsa at its heart. He was a trader and traveller. His journeys took him deep into the Balkans, and it may have been in Ionian

Smyrna, the first centre of the Sabbatean movement, that he chose his path in life. In those years the Judaic archipelago of the Mediterranean and Eastern Europe was still convulsed by the upheavals left in the wake of Sabbatai Zevi, the would-be Messiah who preached a doctrine of profanation, was arrested by the Ottoman authorities, held captive in the Gallipoli fortress and there, in the year 1666, converted to Islam. The various sects that sprang up after his death in exile elaborated a cryptic set of theologies. They contain echoes of Christian belief, intense forebodings of apocalypse and redemption, and a relentless focus on the need to overturn all laws and lay bare all secret doctrines.

A fierce, electric energy courses through the Sabbatean era in Jewish history. It was a time when disputes and rivalries broke out across the face of Europe. Diaspora communities in Spain, Italy, North Africa and the Levant were swept up in these dramas and set on edge. How to explain the apostasy of a Messiah? How to follow a saviour who betrays his faith? The solution found was ingenious. It had a mesmerising logic. So dark was the fallen world that it had become necessary, on this reasoning, for the Messiah to abase himself, to enter the house of darkness, to take on the false religion of the infidel.

The ideas of the medieval Kabbalah were lurking in this script. Simple versions of those ideas are well enough disseminated in our day. They still have a potency, and a poetry, even when removed by translation from their true linguistic field. They stem from the notion that a fall came after the first creation. The primal order of the world has been shattered; it lies in fragments; the sparks of the divine are spread over the expanses of the earth, and it is essential to gather them up, each last scintilla: to go down into the darkness where they are disseminated, down into the furthest reaches of the world, and there embrace sin and falsity. Such paradoxes had a natural appeal in a time when the adherents of the faith were constantly persecuted, when established rituals brought nothing, when God's protection had so manifestly failed. It was this climate of ideas that paved the way for the religious cataclysms ahead.

During his journeyings down the Black Sea coastline, Frank married, in Nikopol in Bulgaria, the daughter of a well-connected merchant. This tie brought him into contact with extreme Sabbatean groups. He was a man of will and charisma: he assumed the leadership of the sect, and proclaimed the new revelation. It was he himself who was the reincarnated Messiah, the pure embodiment of God's power in the world of man. His cult had distinctive, indeed scandalous features: it involved religious orgies, and the mass conversion of his followers to the outward forms of Catholicism.

Frank made a triumphant progress through Podolia and

through the kingdom of Poland, where he engaged in public debates and contestations with leaders of the church. His fame grew rapidly. To control the unrest that spread in his wake he was confined to Częstochowa, where he established a lavish court. With the break-up of the Polish kingdom he moved his entourage to Brno, in the Habsburg lands. He was received in Vienna by the Empress Maria Theresa, and may well have initiated espionage ventures through the South Slav region in concert with her diplomats. Eventually he came under the protection of the German princely house of Ysenburg, and took up residence in the Rhineland town of Offenbach, near Frankfurt. He lived there in great state surrounded by an ever-growing band of acolytes. His daughter Ewa, famous for her beauty and sophistication, was the chatelaine. It was put about, and widely believed, that she was in truth a Romanov princess.

Frank died in December 1791. Europe was in the grip of war and revolution. Behind him he left communities of believers throughout Bohemia, Moravia, the Eastern Marches and the Balkans, and many of the darkest, most nihilistic trends that mark out modern thought seem prefigured in the beliefs he spread.

*

Few today bother very much with Jacob Frank and his visions of disaster, when disaster has been visited upon the borderlands of Europe, and the communities where Frank found his believers are no more—but there are certain exceptions, chief among them the leading twentieth-century scholar of Kabbalistic literature, Gershom Scholem, who was the professor of Jewish mysticism at the Hebrew University, and is known in the wider world for his close friendship with the critic Walter Benjamin. Scholem was strongly drawn to the Sabbatean phase in Jewish history and its aftermath. His most extended piece of writing is a reconstruction of the lives of Sabbatai Zevi and the prophet of the messianic movement, Nathan of Gaza—but it was in one of his much earlier essays that his involvement with the dark absolutes of Frankist thought comes most clearly to the surface of his work.

'Redemption through Sin' was published in a Hebrew journal in 1937, when the shadows were looming over Europe, and Scholem's epistolary and imaginative engagement with the Messiah-like figure of Benjamin was at its height. But Benjamin had chosen the path of dialectical materialism in preference to the Zionist cause. He was by then a well-established freelancer in the orbit of literary communism. He was in exile. His life would end in flight from the Gestapo and suicide: illumination through darkness did not come his way.

Scholem's exploration of Frank begins at the notorious

core of the doctrine, the idea that the secret truths of religion must be exposed, that violation of the law is its truest fulfilment, that the route to the sacred is through the profane. This is the classic antinomian stand: one comprehensible only against a background of disappointments and deepening religious crisis; one born from the tide of pogroms and persecutions then sweeping, as they did so often in the past millennium, through the heartlands of European Jewish settlement—for there must be an oppressor if a religion is turned, in this way, so utterly against itself.

Jacob Frank left an unusual manuscript, the 'Sayings of the Lord'—a heretic's testament, little read in our times, until Scholem plunged deeply into it, and found there vigour, imagination and poetic fire. The picture he paints of the messianic leader has a striking immediacy about it. Scholem had combed through the Frankist doctrines. He ordered them; he gave them a glimmer and a splendour. His 'Redemption through Sin' is not only a masterpiece of theological exegesis—it is a driven, haunted piece of literature as well.

*

And here we come close to the paradox at the heart of religious revolutions. They have the energy of sacrilege. They make the future unstable. They hold out the promise of rebirth. Even to those of a settled temperament the appeal they make is sharp. There could have been no figure more redolent of the established academic world than Scholem, a scholar commanding the airy peaks of his obscure discipline, a porer through manuscripts, a man of the study and the library; and yet his sketch of Jacob Frank is much more than just an ambiguous, half-sympathetic biographic portrait—it is the record of a fascination.

Thus Frank is at once 'one of the most frightening phenomena in the whole of Jewish history' and a figure of tremendous, if satanic, power. He is a strongman, perverting whatever will to truth and goodness remained in the maze-like ruins of the souls of Sabbatean believers. But he also dreamed of reconstructing Jewish national existence, much, indeed, like the Zionists among whom Scholem lived in pre-war Palestine. He is unlettered; he boasts constantly of his own lack of culture—but he displays a talent for 'the pithy, the illustrative, the strikingly symbolic expression'. He is a nihilist, and one of primal ferocity, yet his teachings yield up a genuine creed of life. No sensitive individual, reading the excerpts from his testament, could possibly contemplate them without emotion, says Scholem. There was, in short, a heroic element in him, and this was the pull that drew his adherents. Those who followed him had deliberately chosen to follow a path along which nothing is impossible: 'Here was a man who was not afraid to push on to the very end, to take the final step into the abyss, to drain the cup of desolation and destruction to the lees until the last bit of holiness had been made into a mockery.'

The odd echoes of Christ's Passion on the cross and the prefiguration of the Shoah in Eastern Europe are hard to keep from one's thoughts as passages of this kind occur with increasing frequency in Scholem's synoptic account of Frankist belief, a system conceived specifically to destroy a religion because its God had failed: to profane, to empty out, and by so doing, to trigger—what? A fresh creation? A revelation? A new law? The secret words of a higher faith, lying unread beneath worn letters on old biblical scrolls, hidden in the Ark of the Covenant's black light?

The new Messiah had a dark picture of the cosmos. Our world, he taught, is not God's world. No: it is one made by evil powers, malign angels and demiurges, the beings who brought death among us. The only way to truth is to smash this false world's laws, pollute every religion and every positive system of belief. Here, then, is a message of unrelenting bleakness, which was propagated as secret doctrine among scores of thousands of believers, and held them fast: a belief which lived on for decades, and may even have kept its hold in various Balkan communities well into the century just past. Mankind must go into the pit of darkness, into nothing, and believers must maintain the mystic burden of their silence all through whatever sufferings may come. 'It is better to see than to speak, for the heart must not reveal what it knows to the mouth.'

Understanding, reflection, enlightenment—these, to Frank, were playthings. Conventional religious observance was a waste of time. The pursuit of havoc was his goal. Here is the promise Frank held out in his 'Sayings': 'Wherever Adam trod, a city was built—but wherever I set foot all will be destroyed, for I come into this world only to destroy and to annihilate—but what I build will last forever.' What theology is this, with its dreamlike vision of a remote utopia, when the old order and its sacred words have all been swept away? Is it religion at all? Frank himself provides a brisk, baffling summary: 'It is one thing to worship God—and quite another to follow the path that I have taken.'

At which point, having sketched in the briefest outline some aspects of one of the most perplexing and least-remembered episodes in European religious history, an episode that stands, nevertheless, in strange fashion at the centre of the continent's past, and makes a connecting hinge between the early centuries of Christianity and the age of revolutions, let me swiftly spin the globe, and transport you, far away, again, in time and space.

*

In the summer months of 1937, the same year that Scholem

was completing 'Redemption through Sin' in his book-lined office in a fledgling university in a nation that had not yet come into being, Captain Leo Frobenius, the great impresario of German imperial ethnography, was on holiday at his villa on the shore of Lago Maggiore, planning his last expedition. Frobenius, whose chief interests in life were espionage, absinthe and black women, had conceived the idea that the Kimberley region of northwest Australia could serve him as a window onto the fast-vanishing primeval past of man. Its corpus of rock art of varying styles, which was then being described for the first time by missionary researchers, was the focus of his attention. The relevant permits were obtained. The Frobenius Institute expedition arrived in Broome by circuitous route early the next year. Under the leadership of a young specialist in Aboriginal and Oceanic societies named Helmut Petri, the team then travelled deep inland from Walcott Inlet, through the territories of the Worora and the Ngarinyin.

Their discoveries were spectacular; their timing was poor. They had only just returned to Germany after their lengthy field investigations when war broke out. The frayed ties of academic co-operation between Germany and the English-speaking world were promptly severed. Much of the material Petri and his team had gathered up was destroyed in the Allied bombing raids that razed Frankfurt am Main.

It was only nine years after the end of World War II that Petri was able at last to publish an abbreviated account of his findings.

*Sterbende Welt in Nordwestaustralien* is a production of great beauty, shot through with overtones of mourning and grief. Petri regarded it as no more than a damaged torso, a fragment of the book he planned to write—but that fragmentary quality gives the work much of its force. Although it is ostensibly concerned with ethnographic description of remote tribes and their social adaptations, it is in fact a study of a culture under stress and in collapse, and when I first came across it and made my way through its pages I at once felt it held the key to any truthful understanding of north Australia's first civilisations and their fate.

*Sterbende Welt* is written in a smooth and understated German. It was translated at the insistence of the rock-art scholar Grahame Walsh, who entrusted the task to a notable specialist, Ian Campbell, of the University of New England. That translation offers to an Anglophone readership the unsparing details of what Petri learned and saw: things so disquieting they drew him back to the Kimberley and the desert fringe repeatedly, and made him into a kind of nomad, or pilgrim, constantly haunting the mission settlement of La Grange on the northwest coastline, where the large Aboriginal community of Bidyadanga stands today.

Petri paints a picture of a world in dissolution, but he also records the startling, furious energies of creation at work in the societies he came to know. The established religions of the northwest were failing; new cults of extraordinary vigour were sweeping through. They were imbued with danger; they involved acts of profanation and the speaking of secret words; they had a messianic, despairing edge. Chief among them was the Kurangara, which Petri, like his colleague on the Frobenius expedition Andreas Lommel, understood as a response to the pressures of invasion and colonial subjection. The Kurangara resembles other such cults recorded during the same period across frontier Australia, but the detail with which it is captured in this German text allows us to see into its heart, and see there something critical about the thought-world of Aboriginal north and central Australia—an element that was present in the middle years of the twentieth century and persists in disguised fashion to this day.

*

When Petri began his work, the cult was at its peak and was spreading fast across the Kimberley. It dominated Dampierland and had a firm foothold in the country of the Ngarinyin, the Worora and the Unambal. It was on the march towards the east. But its origins were in the centre, in the deserts, in some imagined pure domain where Aboriginal societies still possessed strength and magic force. It had been brought north by the Djanba, spirits of the inland, creatures of aridity, fearful beings. They lived in the dry heart of the continent. It was there, in distant country, that they kept their subterranean camps. They had emerged from the red soil at the start of time. They were shape-shifters; they knew everything and could do anything; they could travel on the waves of thought, and see for endless distances. The Djanba were fair-skinned, and had long beards, but Kimberley people rarely saw them, for the spirits travelled at speed, leaving no footprints where they walked, not pausing even for a moment's rest. They were most active on moonless nights, or in the haze-tormented midday heat, when their bodies cast no shadows; and they were thirsty—inordinately thirsty—both for water, and for the blood of humankind. Dances, songs, cult objects and potent rituals were associated with these beings, but no one except the adepts of the cult could understand their mysterious desert language.

There are many features of this ritual complex and its associated sexual practices which Petri describes and which I will pass over, but certain other telltale aspects of the Kurangara, provided by Lommel, point to the wellsprings of the cult. Thus it is striking that the Djanba spirits are . described as having horns on their heads just like a bull's horns. When they come into the Kimberley they live in houses of corrugated iron like station homesteads. To hunt they use sticks like rifles. They point them—then thunder sounds, lightning strikes, the earth trembles and everywhere many kangaroos fall dead to the ground. There is an end-of-the-world atmosphere about these anecdotes that must be put down to Christian influence, but the essence of the cult's origins are plain. In the Kurangara the new experiences flowing from the encounter with white civilisation have been transmuted, given artistic form.

Such were the symptoms of crisis and dislocation Petri found awaiting him—signs that spoke of revolution in the realm of belief and God. It is clear that there is a two-fold movement under way: resistance, and co-option. Defiance, and surrender to the seductive play of influence. The German ethnographers, who were watching this tableau unfold before them even as a deathly cult swept through their own world, knew very well what they were witnessing: the end of an epoch, a time of dreadful instability, the first seeds of a new accommodation being sown. They realised that the sacred never vanishes. It flows, wave-like, through men's lives, moving smoothly from form to form.

Lommel saw these shifts through the prism of psychology. He felt the Aboriginal societies of the Kimberley needed a living, strong magical atmosphere. A magic cult gave people a spiritual focal point outside themselves. Without such an atmosphere total disintegration, a great spiritual disorder and disorientation, must occur.

Petri, for his part, grasped the essence of the phenomenon almost at an instinctual level. Perhaps it needed an outsider's eyes to diagnose the process. 'It is a well-known fact,' he wrote, 'that European colonization upset the spiritual equilibrium of the Australian Aborigines.' The religious compact at the heart of life had failed. The relationship between the generations had been overthrown. The young, seeing the white world in all its destructive potency, had lost faith in their own traditions, but the workings of western civilisation were impenetrable to them. They found in the spirits of the new cults the inner support that old beliefs could no longer give.

How to miss the lurking pattern? Millenarian cults and religious uprisings share a straightforward grammar. The old law fails. It is overturned, a new law is preached, and that law is founded on the shock of sudden revelations. It will tend to borrow elements from the oppressive, threatening new master-power abroad in the world. It adapts, it assimilates, it resists—it proclaims year zero, and awaits a dawn.

*

This pattern, when it appears in Australian frontier history, as it has often, is rarely seen for what it is, for that frontier is viewed and understood through mainstream eyes—and our picture of past events in both the deserts and the tropical and savannah country is a picture freighted down by sentiment and perspective bias. Few frontier dwellers and specialists in the area really understand that the frontier has another side. Few historians of the inland and the encounters that have occurred over the past two centuries against that backdrop realise that men and women in traditional societies still half expect non-indigenous Australians to leave their country at some point, when certain ritual cycles are complete. For outsiders in the bush do not, on the whole, think magically, or see the ceremonial logic of that world and the compelling force it exerts upon those plunged within it.

The ideas western observers apply to the Aboriginal realm come, rather, from social-science and cultural frameworks. They are the ideas of the bohemian, the intellectual, the aid worker or the enlightened functionary, and they bring confusion in their wake. The first generations of incomers in the remote world were much better equipped— the missionaries, with their belief in divine providence, were on the same wavelength as the tribal groups they moved among and were at pains to convert, and the relative harmony and happiness of the missionary era may well be largely due to this confluence of understandings and views of life. Two generations ago that system of frontier management fell into abeyance. Another order was imposed, an administrative order, elaborate, with constantly shifting priorities.

It was at this very point that one of the most widely studied and most elusive interactions between traditionally accented Aboriginal society and mainstream Australia unfolded—the Western Desert art movement, which was born in Papunya settlement nearly forty-five years ago, and it is to this landscape, this remote community grandly set in the folds of the purple Ulumbara range, that I transport you now.

*

The foundation story of the painting movement is well entrenched, and widely known. The presiding genius was a young, highly strung, artistically inclined teacher named Geoffrey Bardon, who encouraged a group of men he had encountered during his brief stay at Papunya to paint their traditional designs—at first in the form of a mural on the schoolhouse wall, then on small boards and scraps of masonite. This activity was taken up. It became popular with a number of the men, who poured out a set of complex images. Word of their paintings spread through the neighbouring settlements of the desert region.

The news ignited intense controversy. Fierce conflicts over this disclosure of sacred emblems and its likely consequences began. Those disputes lasted for several years, until a solution was devised: dots and linear patterns were used by the painters to mask the secret symbols on their boards and canvases; and, as with Kafka's parable of the leopards in the ancient temple, soon those surface decorations became the heart of the work.

The outside taste for the art of the desert slowly grew. The visual vocabulary of the painting men was transmitted across Australia—dots, circles, radiating lines—it is a familiar part of the cultural landscape today. Large exhibitions in state galleries routinely tell triumphalist versions of this story, replete with odd, almost messianic overtones: the humble origins, the slow advance, the accelerating acceptance of indigenous work, the final storming of the high-art citadel.

\*

What was the true nature of this foundation episode? What transpired in those first days when art flowered at Papunya? There is the standard, 'official' account, as given in a hundred vapid art catalogues. The Aboriginal understanding is quite different. Those who were present and remember those weeks at Papunya recall that when the mural of the honey-ant design was first sketched out on the school wall a wail of lamentation sounded through the settlement. There was a degree of coercion involved. It was a time of grief: sacred symbols had been shown to outside eyes.

But that was, in some sense, the point. It was not simply, or not only, a story of oppression; it was yet another fluid frontier episode, ambiguous in the extreme—and the more I turn over in my thoughts that time, so near to us, so shrouded by the veils of testimonial narratives, the more it seems to me that we should view it as a further instance of upheaval in the realm of belief. This sequence of events, so pivotal for Australia's new conception of the national story, so central to the culture's self-reflection in art—can we not see it in the same light as the Sabbatean and the Kurangara dramas, as a gesture of religious rebellion, born of defiance and of despair?

It was an act, above all, of revelation. The artists were displaying their designs; they were profaning them. There they were, poised on the frontier between worlds, between two times, testing the powers of creation. For Bardon, it was a blissful experience of artistic fulfilment; for the painters, an experience of holy dread, when things held secret since the world's creation were uncovered, one by one. There were complex expectations in mind. Perhaps westerners would now recognise the grandeur of the symbols stretched out before them, and the domain of thought and ritual they brought to life. Perhaps some new compact of more even-handed association might be possible between the different peoples in the landscape. Perhaps ancestral powers would be stirred, and the face of the desert would be transformed. But one thing the first painters and their associates among the senior men at Papunya could not have anticipated is the large-scale pursuit by outsiders of their sacred knowledge—a pursuit we now see in full cry.

How multiplicit the ironies have become! The first symbol paintings made in the desert in 1971 fitted neatly into the category of ethnographic art. Their deeper meanings were little studied. Today, they are priceless treasures, and much contemporary desert work is viewed, at least in Australia, as fine art, of permanent significance, worthy of detailed attempts at scholarly interpretation. As a result, a vast research effort is under way to uncover and record as much Aboriginal tradition as can be extracted from its custodians, and this campaign is heavily backed by museums, universities and cultural institutions.

There is both prestige and monetary value to be gained from the brokerage of Aboriginal culture, that culture the first painters at Papunya dreamed of revitalising and keeping strong. It has been greatly weakened in the intervening decades, by the familiar suspects—television, welfare, drugs and alcohol—but also by a sense that its secrets are gone and its sacred power has begun to fade. The outsiders who watch that world and expend their affections on it know. They can tell; and there is a deepening conviction among them that what lies behind work of such beauty must not be allowed to vanish. It must be archived, transcribed, saved. Hence the data transfer: a last-chance gold rush, as art historians, anthropologists and culture theorists rush to map the contours of indigenous beliefs. Western scholars like to portray this as 'two-way' research, respectful collaboration, a product of intercultural understanding. But given the hieratic nature of the ritual that underlies much desert culture, this appetite for 'inside' knowledge about paintings and their subject matter creates a tension between the makers of the art and the would-be interpreters of their work.

That stress line has been sharpening over recent years. It is a new version of the same fault line that opens up when the sacred is in play. We are back: back on the frontier. Worlds clash. Beliefs break. They are shattered, then swiftly reshaped. The forces that undo them can come in very different guises. The persecutions of Eastern Europe; the sweeping land seizures under way in north Australia's first pastoral decades, when all was guns and violence; the invasive encouragements of the modern Aboriginal art market, as well. The secret realm of desert ritual was breached more than four decades ago. The pressure from outside has only grown since.

This creates dilemmas for its guardians. They have learned a strange lesson: that love can be the most disruptive force of all. These questions are much discussed by desert men, above all by men from the Pitjantjatjara language region of South Australia. They were the chief critics of the first disclosure of traditional designs in the early 1970s, and their remote country is the final target of the knowledge quest.

Here is Frank Young, from Amata community, touching on these themes, describing the power in men's paintings, and the dangers caught up in traditional art: he is speaking in Pitjantjatjara, a language of stripped-back precision and elegance. '*Tjukurpa kumpilpa tjuta putu Anangu tjutangku tjakultjunanyi canvas-tjangka munu putu tjakultjunanyi panya Tjukurpa pulka mulapa ngaranyi kumpilpa Tjukurpa unngutja Anangu tjutaku.*'

Something comes through, even in a translation of his words: 'There are things in the canvases people cannot talk about because the sacred Tjukurpa is really deeply inside us—it is us.'

Of course Mr Young is speaking here for the old traditions. Of course he is trying to redraw the sacred line. Of course he is pleading for a degree of secrecy—but once the first transgression has been made, once the sacred, that quicksilver, has been put in play, you can never tell where it will go.

It is always receding in our world. It is always present, like the background shell of radiation from the day the universe began. It is constantly coming into being and constantly being extinguished. Its essence is to be beyond reach, beyond stable form, a gleam, a fire in the bush, a mirage of water on the horizon's edge—and this was brought home to me forcefully in the course of a brief journey, now some years in the past, which I made with a pair of desert men from the remote community of Karilywara, John Ward and Mr Giles: two men who were complete in themselves, and poised in their worlds of thought; two men whom I had long felt close to and admired.

It was the hot, stormy season in their country. They wanted to head west, both to inspect the distant rock-hole site of Tartjar and to visit the ranges in its vicinity. They had the desire; I had the Toyota four-wheel-drive, already in a state of near collapse after a series of imprudent transits down the back tracks of the Gibson Desert. I also had a broken arm, but this injury was of no concern to them, though it was in the forefront of my thoughts. Changing flat tyres had been proving something of a problem, and I had the odd sense that I was encountering a wide range of similarly wounded desert creatures—limping bush turkeys, hawks fluttering on the roadway with broken wings. Were they portents? Were they protective beings?

We headed off. We passed the hill of the porcupine, where some of the desert's most intense wild tobacco grows. We left the tracks behind. All round us the plumes of vast bushfires were rising, their smoke columns stained dust-red by the sunset's gleam. Night fell. We drove on—to my great surprise. I had long since internalised the western wisdom that old desert men like to be in their swags by sundown, and fear the dark.

'Keep going,' they chorused. 'Keep going: it's close.'

'You're not afraid?' I said. 'Afraid—of the spirits out here?'

'I am a spirit,' said Mr Giles, rather disconcertingly. 'So is Mr Ward. You know that.'

'I do?'

'Yes,' they both said, very firmly. '*Yuwai!* We control the water, the rain and the fire—they're ours. You know all that.'

We ground our way in low gear across a sudden ridge, and down. There, right in front, was the rock hole, full of water, shining in the night. We stopped. We clambered out, and as we stood there, suddenly a shooting star plunged across the sky, gleaming and flaring as it fell and the different layers of its surface were burned up. I counted: one, two, three, four, five. I half felt I could hear those detonations in the silence, reaching me across the distance and the dark— and at once the two men beside me began singing, in low, rhythmic voices, together, singing in old, high language, a chant that went on, rising, sinking. They were staring up towards the sky where the star had fallen, tears in their eyes, their chests heaving up and down. They were singing with all their might.

I listened as their voices filled the dark around me, and it came to me how little I grasped of their world and its structure. Nothing. I had never heard them say a single word about the stars, and the sky, and how they might be sacred—though they are sacred in every culture where men look up at the great silence of the overarching night. They are the screen where we most clearly see the scale of the cosmos, and the slightness of our world, all our dreams and loves and fondest thoughts—and realise in the same instant that those thoughts and dreams are all we have.

But even as I form this idea it occurs to me that the one western study of the desert world written truly on Aboriginal terms touches often on this realm. C. P. Mountford's *Nomads of the Western Desert* is an exorbitant production, full of images captioned purely in terms of their local meaning. Thus a photograph of a stone headland might be listed as 'a basking perentie in the sun'. Interspersed throughout the mazy chapters of the narrative are stories of the stars and sky—and it may well be this, as much as its depictions of a handful of sacred places, that led to the withdrawal from sale of *Nomads* on cultural grounds shortly after its publication in the year of the author's death, 1976, since when it has been sunk in deep obscurity, little looked at, hard to find.

It took me years of searching before I tracked down a copy in that centre of intellectual contraband North Terrace, Adelaide. It was a dishevelled first edition, with a broken spine, its pages torn and creased and stained here and there by reddish sand. It had clearly been the prized possession of a desert community, though it had begun its life in the Upper Goulburn regional library system, and made its way through several stages to my hands.

I pored over it with the attention Gershom Scholem gave his manuscripts, looking for shards of secret knowledge there, and coming on brief mentions of the constellations and the glowing, pulsing southern stars—and at those moments my mind would leap back to the time of my childhood, in the Tatras, when I used to walk the slopes towards the Skalnaté Pleso observatory by night, alone, gazing upwards at the great arc of the Milky Way. And I would be back at once at the beginning of my journey, beneath the quicksilver of youthful skies.

# III

# Words and Nature

The Russian film director Andrei Tarkovsky, a deliberate and painstaking artist, went to great lengths to include in his late work *Stalker*, almost as its centrepiece, an elaborately composed tracking shot—a camera movement that captured many of the enigmas we face, today, in reflecting on the place of nature in our subjugated world.

So precise was his eye, and so telling were the images he succeeded in crystallising, in those few screen moments, that I should like to sketch something of the story of this film, its creation, and the intuitions and ideas behind it: ideas that light up our shared task, as writers and readers staring at the face of nature. But I would like to proceed from this beginning indirectly, in a mazy, elliptical fashion, by means of an answering set of stories, stories which come from the heart of the Australian landscape, a world as distant as can be from the wide forests of Russia and Northern Europe, a world with rhythms of its own—the deep bush and the rangelands, the deserts of the centre and the west. And perhaps these brief tales will hang together, like the distinct movements in a suite of music, and illuminate each other, and even suggest some ways we may learn to look, and listen, unconditionally when we approach the natural world. It is not my aim to draw them to some fierce and willed conclusion, so much as to let them stand side by side, and send shafts of implication between their various narratives, as if mirroring the way that influences pass between the landscape's order and the world of man.

Here, then, is my starting point for this meditation: one of the more mysterious films made by a most mysterious director, who was regarded as both genius and fool, who was praised and hounded, who believed in the splendour of the natural kingdom and constantly lost himself inside its beauties.

*Stalker*, which was made under the Soviet Union's studio system, in 1979, with limited resources, tells a science-fiction tale, in stylised fashion: the stalker of the title is a professional guide who leads two pilgrims into a forbidden Zone where the laws of nature have been modified, as a result of some past cataclysm. The realm they travel through is an industrial wasteland: there are decaying, half-destroyed buildings, weed-covered bunkers, rivers thick with foaming pollutants. At the centre of the Zone, and hard of access, is a single room, where one's heart's desires can be fulfilled.

The making of the film was a disaster: the crew spent the whole of their first year shooting the outdoor scenes, but they were using experimental Kodak stock, quite unfamiliar to Soviet laboratories. It was damaged in the development process, and had to be discarded: the project was begun again from scratch. Tarkovsky had found a striking location for his cinematic parable. He filmed the core sequence at a deserted hydroelectric station on the Jägala River, near Tallinn, the capital of Estonia—at that time a constituent republic of the Soviet Union.

A handful of landscape shots showed panoramic views of the nearby Iru power plant's cooling tower, and left the viewer with the strong impression that some nuclear mishap lay behind the creation of the Zone—and so deeply was this idea ingrained in the imagination of the Soviet-era movie-going public that when the Chernobyl nuclear-power station in the Ukraine exploded in April 1986, scattering radiation plumes across large parts of Eastern Europe, the first scouts to brave the plant's wrecked periphery began referring to themselves as 'stalkers' on their return from the burnt-out reactor's desolate surrounds.

For all Tarkovsky's enduring fame as a director, the film

is hard to notch up as a success. Its plot is gossamer-thin, its acting performances wooden, its dialogue near farcical. The visual language is what sets it apart: the constant travelling shots that focus on the scarred concrete, the mud and dirt, the rusted scatters of machinery, the undergrowth of livid green. Those shots have their distinctive rhythm, much like the repeated birdcalls and the wind gusts caught on the soundtrack; they oblige the viewer to stare at the minutest details in the landscape: fragments, broken fragments of the world. Indeed there is nothing intact in the film's Zone, and yet the journey through it, down its hidden pathways, amid its waiting ordeals and dangers, becomes a journey into the heart of life.

The emblematic tracking shot Tarkovsky placed at the centre of the film dwells not on the faces of his characters, nor on the sky or clouds. It, too, focuses on what has been demolished and destroyed; the camera's eye moves above the waterlogged floor of an abandoned building: this is the antechamber to the magic 'room' where all wishes will be answered. The water has swept over a tiled and decorated surface: plant fronds stream through it; there is a submerged metallic object, which bears a resemblance to a prayer-scroll container; there is the torn image of an icon; there are tiny schools of fish in sinuous motion. It is such images as these, rather than the philosophical exchanges between the characters, that linger in the mind.

But today, nearly four decades after it was filmed, and long after the final collapse of the Soviet system under which it was made, *Stalker*, like the other films of Tarkovsky, which are in truth all linked components in a single filmic meditation, speaks in changed voice. What now, when the art film as a form has died: what are we to think of such a slow and solemn unfolding of images and ideas on screen? What are we to think of the director's view of threatened nature, or of his evident conviction that divine tokens lurk in the landscape, or of the sense of fatal foreboding that industrial-power complexes awoke in his heart?

Soon after the completion of *Stalker*, Tarkovsky left the Soviet Union, and never returned. In his last years he was afflicted by lung cancer, the disease that was also to claim his wife, Larissa, and his favourite actor, Anatoly Solonitsyn. Solonitsyn was exceptionally close to Tarkovsky, and took the lead role in several of his films, including *Stalker*. This coincidence has led to speculation that the making of *Stalker*, and the choice of set for the Zone, proved fatal for all three— and indeed there are only a few members of the film's first location crew who are still alive today. Vladimir Sharun, the sound designer for the production, recalled his experiences with Tarkovsky in a reminiscence for the newspaper *Komsomolskaya Pravda* in 2001:

We were shooting near Tallinn in an area
around the River Pirita with a half-functioning
hydroelectric station. Up the river was a chemical
plant and it poured out poisonous liquids. There
is even this shot in *Stalker*: snow falling in the
summer and white foam floating down the river.
In fact it was some horrible poison.

During his brief spell in Western Europe as a director
in exile, Tarkovsky collaborated on a documentary with his
Italian friend Tonino Guerra: its key exchanges were filmed
outdoors, in a verdant landscape, with Tarkovsky lounging
against a tree, almost as if he felt the desire to become one
with its trunk and bark, and it is in this posture that he
sets out his ideas about nature, art and life—how beauty
lies in the balance of parts in a composition, how art is only
necessary to us because we seek harmony in an imperfect
world. We have no harmony: if we lived in such a state, art
would be pointless; the urge to make it would pass away. This
leads him to his ideas about the aims of art, and those ideas,
the ideas of a man who felt light's flow could reveal the play
of time, may resonate with our circumstances today, when
such a superfluity of creative projects surrounds us, and the
point of this rich banquet seems ever more obscure.

Art, says Tarkovsky, is not about finding out about the
world. No: knowledge limits us; it distracts us from our main

purpose in life. The more we know, the less we know: getting deeper, our horizons become narrower. As was clear even to his colleagues in Soviet times, Tarkovsky was a man of faith: his attention to the natural order stemmed from his sense that the spirit of the creation could be found lurking in its humblest parts; he was not a taxonomist of plants, or trees; the flow of streams and rivers held no interest for him; what captivated him was the hidden pulse and depth of life he felt he could make out, in all its patterned, fateful splendour, in the images he filmed—even the slightest, most transitory things—the gleam of sunshine on running water's surface, the waving of pale seed heads in the wind, the dim light on flaked paintwork inside silent buildings.

The tracking shot at the heart of *Stalker*, moving slowly above the submerged floor, with its icons and its emblems, picks out a torn-off day marker from a calendar: it bears the date of 28 December seven years after the filming; that day was the last full day Tarkovsky spent on Earth. The inscription on his gravestone at the Russian cemetery of Sainte-Geneviève-des-Bois in Paris reads: 'To the man who saw the angel.'

In the course of his life Tarkovsky saw many things, but one thing he could not see was what time would do to him. Over the past three decades, the very idea of making high-art films on such a scale has almost vanished, together with the

Cold War, the confrontation between rival cultural blocs and the notion of prestige state-studio productions designed to serve as emblems of the progressive order. If the crisis of ideologies that once shadowed our whole world has passed, so too has the appetite for such grandly conceived, symbol-laden cinema, just as the mood has changed for writing.

The vogue now is for entertainment, sensation, genre, storytelling on the intimate scale, and for visual narratives that strive to capture the fine grain of individual experience. If a landscape of the kind Tarkovsky set at the centre of his works appears on screen today, it is as likely to be digitised as to be the product of immersion in the heart of the natural world. The emotional charge of the natural order shown on the screen has changed as well: no longer is nature viewed as a distinct realm, the place where man's sway stops, and older laws prevail; nature is a threatened world, a subset of man's dominion, a place to be pitied and preserved—and this shift transforms the way we see mid-twentieth-century films made in a landscape setting, and lends them a nostalgic tone they did not initially possess.

Tarkovsky's films appeared in the West, to great acclaim, in the 1970s and 1980s. I remember going to see them at late-night rerun cinemas in European capitals, and admiring them, in the way one admires, when young, the things one knows one should admire, even though the lengthy depictions of the natural world in each film in turn left me puzzled: why such passionate fondness for the streams and meadows and silver-birch forests of the Russian hinterland? I had not yet found a direct pathway into the landscape: a landscape that could be an active presence, more than a stage-set. The nature I had in my thoughts in those years was neutral: if it was beautiful, it was also embellished with ideas, above all the idea of the romantic sublime; it was a space where man's imagination was free to roam.

But, for Tarkovsky, nature was transcendent, and for multiple reasons: not only was the Russian landscape imbued with the breath of life; it was also a symbol of resistance to the Kremlin regime, and this aspect of his films, which westerners sensed only dimly, was instantly apparent to Soviet audiences. The sheer act of singling out the features of the natural world was enough—the bark of trees, plant blossoms, horses in the fields, the light filtered by the changing motions of the clouds—sequences of shots treating such things were instantly understood as subversive. They were not friendly to the communist state's great goals; they did not celebrate the large-scale exploitation of the natural kingdom; they did not show crop-covered countryside dotted by combine harvesters, or excavators dragging their chains across a stepped and tiered mine open-cut—and it was precisely because of this choice of imagery that the distribution of Tarkovsky's films in his own country proved so problematic, and that he lived such an austere and straitened life.

In retrospect, it seems ever clearer that one of his principal subjects was the fate of the Russian countryside, and the entire continent stretching east beyond the Urals: a vast wilderness, punctuated only by mining and engineering centres, criss-crossed by exiguous highways and unending rail lines. When summoning these long, symphonic films to mind today, it is hard to recall their fierce quality of dissent: yet their treatment of their subject matter, which once seemed vital only to dissidents and internal opponents of the Soviet system, has gained a relevance in the wider world. The nature Tarkovsky depicted as under threat is under threat everywhere.

There is, for instance, a disquieting parallel between the landscape of the Soviet Union and the landscape of the Australian continent: both large, resource-rich, increasingly exploited, their inland reaches occupied chiefly by the residents of mining centres and remote indigenous communities. The location set selected for *Stalker*, in the vicinity of Tallinn, now forms part of a prosperous and independent European state, and much of the wasteland Tarkovsky filmed has been carefully rehabilitated. But it would be very easy to remake *Stalker* today in an equally baroque and devastated landscape in the Australian northwest—in the Pilbara, at once the grandest, most majestic stretch of country in the desert zone and the most transformed by human hand. How many perfect sets exist for such a film: the loading cantilevers at Finucane Island, the salt piles on the road into Hedland, the ruins on the beach at Condon, the gouged-out deposits at Shay Gap.

For half a century, the Pilbara's iron-ore mines have been worked; the trains have crossed the landscape; the towns have grown; and much the same pattern can be seen in the goldfields: townships, road trains, haul trucks, tailing dams. So it is in North East Arnhem Land, and within the national park at Kakadu; so, too, on the west coast of Cape York, and the Kimberley. The increase in mining and resource development in the far north and centre over the past decades has changed that landscape's character. And what remains of the wild, the bush, if it endures only on our own terms, in a few delimited areas we lock up? What value do we place on those areas we keep, as against the regions we destroy? What presences are still there, for us, in the desert, and the remote bush, in the condition we find them today?

When I was growing up, I knew a good deal, like most people, about the bush, from books, and photographs, and even brief trips and journeys out, into the north, and into the rural hinterlands of Victoria and Queensland—and I knew what I was supposed to make of this landscape lurking around the cities. I knew of its half-achieved domestication and its inherent dangers, its monotony and its fundamental dryness—so it was something of a surprise when I began travelling through the western deserts, and found myself insistently struck by the rapidity and subtlety of the variations in the country: sky, trees, dunes, plants; how changeable they were; how strongly they invited the eye to read them, to trace their patterns, to write their narrative.

You could imagine the landscape as a kind of tale, or musical composition, or as a shifting, elaborately plotted film; and soon, as this affinity became more evident to me, and more persuasive, I began seeking out not just books from the inland but films as well, early films above all, that showed the natural world as it had been decades into the past: newsreels, features, documentaries—*Mailman of the Birdsville Track*, *Where Dead Men Lie*—I would gaze into their flickering flows of images as if the pulse of light and dark inside the camera could take one back in time.

In due course I came across *Desert People*, a detailed account of the life lived in the mid-1960s by a nomad group in the vicinity of Patjarr rock hole. *Desert People* was made by the director Ian Dunlop, for the Commonwealth Film Unit; and though it stays within the conventions of the documentary form, it is a film that pays close attention to the look and texture of the landscape; it captures the country by capturing the behaviour of the people living in it. Its slow, overlapping shots build into a punctilious record: hunting, seed-gathering, winnowing in coolamons; the interactions of a single family, followed for days on end, seemingly alone in a broad stretch of desert.

Even now, when so many films detailing Aboriginal life have been made, and hardly a community in the remote centre remains without its own embedded media unit, churning out sophisticated mementoes of each dance festival and sports weekend, Dunlop's short black-and-white film stands out: it is austere, and measured; its form seems exceptionally well matched to the life of its subjects. *Desert People* won the first prize at a festival of scientific films in Padua, and was even shown in Sydney on short-run commercial release. Dunlop became increasingly prominent in his chosen field; he worked extensively on ethnographic projects in tropical north Australia; but the desert stayed vivid in his mind.

Years later, in a lengthy interview, he described how he had felt a sense of communion with nature there, 'a huge sense of freedom'. He felt a love for the Western Desert: he recalled it in the most precise, specific fashion, as if Aboriginal ways of looking at the world had sunk in on him. What he chiefly remembered about the country he had filmed in was 'the sparseness of it: in the desert everything is important, each clump of spinifex, each flower, each wind ripple, each animal track over the sand assumes great importance and great beauty.' Untouched nature!

For all this, there was a high degree of artifice involved in the making of *Desert People*. Its simplicity was the result of the most elaborate planning and design. This back-story figures in an engaging memoir written by Bob Verburgt, one of the Commonwealth patrol officers responsible for overseeing the western deserts in those days when the nomadic life was coming to its end. *They Called Me 'Tjampu-Tjilpi'* recounts the standard quota of bush adventures, but there is a quiet note of melancholy in the narrative, which is replete with strange encounters and peculiar events.

Verburgt describes his meeting with Dunlop in Adelaide, and their convoy journey out from Alice Springs, in a party that included a sound engineer, a cinematographer and two interpreters. Five days later, after passing through Warburton mission, they reached the country where Verburgt had made contact, some months before, with the nomad family the team hoped to find once again, and film. 'I went on and started a fire in a spinifex-covered gully. Soon I had a smoke rising several hundred feet into the air. Late that afternoon an answering smoke was seen roughly five miles to the west of our position.'

And so the subjects and the makers of *Desert People* approached each other, cautious, slow. Verburgt endeavoured to explain the workings of the camera to the nomad group; he showed them still photographs he had taken at their previous encounter. All seemed set—but things in the bush rarely go to plan. Verburgt's advice to the film crew to secure their belongings went unheeded. On the crew's first night camped out, dingos stole their shoes, as well as a crucial exposure meter housed in a leather case, which was eventually recovered some while later, rather the worse for wear. After the first two days of filming, one of the old men in the nomad group told Verburgt he had fallen sick: the lens of the camera was like an eye staring at him; the motor running film through the machine was like a monster's growl.

Of these upsets, there is no trace at all in the finished film, which has the calm perfection of a descending fugue: wind blows through the landscape, giving the leaves and grasses a constant motion; the characters perform their daily tasks in unhurried manner, almost lost against the wide, bare horizon. At the time, those involved in the project recognised something of its significance. They believed no film crew would ever be in a position to record such lives again. And in the decades since, those expectations have been borne out. The last few desert dwellers have made their way into remote communities. The camps and rock holes in the back country are silent today. Marauding camels tear up the sparse vegetation. There are few other signs of life.

But *Desert People* has also been greatly changed by time's passage. It is a film plunged, now, in the past's depths. It does not show a vanishing realm any more: its entire world has gone. Almost all the individuals the crew filmed are long since dead: though, as chance would have it, one of them died not a decade ago, and he lived a life of unusual, emblematic prominence.

This was Ian Ward, the little boy in the film, whose mother chose his European name in honour of his brief association with Dunlop. He became a leader in the Ngaanyatjarra community of Warburton; he stood out among his own people and in the mainstream; he was a man of clear thought and strong will. But there was a dark, despairing edge to his assessment of his people's place in the world, and it came eventually to predominate. Grief and sadness shadowed him, and they were on his trail on Australia Day in 2008, when he was detained after a random breath test by police in Laverton, a mining township on the desert fringe. From there he was conveyed the next morning in a run-down corrective-services van with faulty air-conditioning the 360 kilometres to Kalgoorlie, but he was near-unconscious by the journey's end, and was never revived: the autopsy found that he had been cooked to death. After his childhood in a world quite measureless, and his brief encounter with the recording camera's lens, he had gained a fate: he was fixed forever; he had entered time.

There is much more to tell about those days when western eyes first came to the rock-hole site of Patjarr, which is also known, almost interchangeably, as Karilywara—but the most striking aspect of its history is the way that different worlds have constantly been colliding there. Mainstream and indigenous experiences and ways of seeing, exploration stories and post-colonial revisions, the struggles of ecologists and of Ngaanyatjarra leaders: everything comes into play; everyone is drawn by the country into speaking, writing, painting—there are images and words strewn through the landscape.

Dunlop and his team were filming, in fact, in the aftermath of a series of rather more bookish, intellectual field trips, when Verburgt accompanied well-known figures from the world of anthropology, such as Norman Tindale and John Greenway, both of whom wrote extensively about their visits; and one prominent American researcher, Richard Gould, even embedded himself for several months with the same family group, before producing an ethnographic portrait of their lives, *Yiwarra: Foragers of the Western Desert*. It was published in the United States, in a dust jacket of bright, disquieting green, and was promptly banned by the council at Warburton because of the photographs of secret initiation rituals included in the text. Yet, despite this transgression, *Yiwarra* is a work of mournful splendour that catches a great deal of the mood of the desert, its landscapes and the sense Gould felt of a world defined by its people, the nature of whose presence there was soon to undergo the most dramatic change. Few people in Australia have seen, let alone read, *Yiwarra*—it is a book that somehow seems to disappear. I owned a copy once, and I hid it so effectively I have never been able to rediscover its place of concealment, but I still remember the quality of its final sentences, and the impression they conveyed of an author who had come to a state of internal balance with the desert and with its receding past.

Shortly after my first reading of *Yiwarra*, and my discovery of *Desert People*, I was able to make some journeys of my own north from Warburton Ranges to the small community set up at Patjarr, in the southeast corner of the Gibson Desert Nature Reserve—and I too came to know that landscape round the rock hole, which has more the appearance of a long, still stretch of river than a soakage or a spring or dam. Those visits, though they were visits to men and women with whom I scarcely had a common language, became a large part of my life in the years when I was first making my way through the western deserts: and for all the dreamlike properties of the country, and the life there, they brought me into the landscape; they remain vivid in my memory today.

They endure: what gave rise to them fades. For, during the past two decades, much has changed in that small society: illnesses, upheavals, fatal accidents; the cycle rushes on; and as a result of these great sadnesses, piled one on top of the next in swift succession, a number of the people who once spent their time there have moved away.

But I still often see one of the women I knew best at the old community. She lives at the Yeperenye Hostel, now, in Alice Springs: her need for renal-dialysis treatments obliges her to live in town, far from her own country—and when our paths cross, we think back to the days when we would drive through the bush on long trips together, north, into the depths of the Gibson; or when I would trail after her on long walks through the country west of Patjarr: she used to lead the way, at a fast, determined pace, striding ahead, for what seemed like hours at a stretch—then, abruptly, she would stop, and grip her iron crowbar tight and start to probe the sand for lizard burrows; or she would look for bush fruits to gather up, or kneel to check for signs that honey ants might be nearby; and on those excursions with her, I found myself paying more attention to the grain and detail of the landscape: each blade of spinifex, each shadow, each bird, each insect track. From time to time, she would pause, in the shade of a desert oak, or by the bank of a dry creek, and talk about her late husband, a Pintupi artist of whom she was extremely proud: she would pull out a faded, crumpled photograph of him from her purse, and display it, then smile, and trace out the patterns of his most famous paintings on the burning sand; then she would shrug, and that was the signal to head back home.

Those forays had a strong influence on me: on the way that I would read the bush. Often as I was driving the long road between Patjarr and the outposts of the western world, I became aware that the way I saw the country round me had been shifting, that I was looking at things differently; I had begun to pick out and distinguish the individual components of the landscape and the sky in fine detail. Above all I remember one evening, around sunset, as I was driving down the old Gunbarrel Highway, south, to Warburton, amid storms. There was a large bushfire burning, far off to the west, behind the ranges. The reflected glow from its flames lit up the clouds. The veils of rainfall drifting earthwards were stained blood-red; each element of that complex scene hung before my eyes in a perfect, otherworldly focus, quite unlike anything I would have been able to see before, or hold inside myself—it was a composed image, resolved; I am tempted to say almost cinematic.

The track led on. The turn-off came: the Great Central Road. A few dips and ridges more, and I could see the lights of Warburton. I slowed, and cruised in, dodging the dog packs. In the low-slung besser-block house where I was staying, just across from the Native Title Unit, I found a friend of mine, Andrei, an artist who was on a desert quest-journey of his own. He was emptying his exiguous backpack. He was unshaven, and pale.

'I just had a very strange experience,' he said. 'I've driven across from Wingellina—I was thinking about it all the way along the road.'

'So you must have come to some conclusions,' I said. 'Tell me about it!'

I settled back. It was a striking tale. He had been staying with a friend of his, a nurse, who was also an aspiring artist and film-maker—and each evening, after work, it was their habit to head out of the community on short drives, to watch the sun go down, and look for locations where they might make their great desert film one day. Once, on the back track that leads past Surveyor General's Corner, they had found a large outstation, quite deserted, its neon lights glowing like a stage-set in the murk; once they came on old, deep mine-workings from the days when lone prospectors were digging for chrysoprase. But this time they drove north for a good half hour, to a set of rocks with a westward view. They were off the little track. They scraped up the ridge: the troop carrier caught on a rock.

'And we were trapped, completely,' said Andrei. 'It

happened very fast, everything. The sun went down. We looked behind us; we lifted up the seats: nothing; there was no jack there. Someone had taken it. And then we realised we had no water. It became clear instantly. I understood—how serious things were. I had to laugh. Laugh at us, at the way we live. You plan, you plan everything, and some detail you can't guess at steals up. And then almost at once, as I thought that, a dreadful weariness spread through me. My arms were tired, and heavy; my head ached, I was numb, I could scarcely walk. Suddenly my throat was dry and parched, the air was hot, and humid—I had a desperate need for water. I wanted to lie down right there on the ground, on the red rocks, lie down, and cradle and rest my head—every instinct to fight and live had gone. I wasn't frightened. I felt a kind of clarity, quite unlike anything I'd felt before. It was the point of dusk. The light was soft; it was as if there were threads of silk light linking everything around us. I could make out every blade of the spinifex grass, every stunted leaf on the bushes, every crack and groove on the bark of the corkwood trees. The whole world had an order, a completeness, like a perfect piece of music.'

'An epiphany! What then?'

'Well,' he said, 'we got out of it, of course, or I wouldn't be here telling you. We looked under the seats again, and there was a lone crowbar there: one of the old ladies must have left it behind after hunting. We wedged it beneath the wheel; we drove off. And then we doubled round. We cut our old wheel tracks somehow, and followed them. When we reached the community they were already thinking about coming after us. We would have been fine. It was just one of those panics. Still, I couldn't help thinking of my namesake, and what went through his mind, at Austerlitz.'

'Your namesake?'

'You're always saying how much you care about Russian literature, and here we are: your first big test, and you don't know anything! Prince Andrei, of course, in *War and Peace*— when he's wounded: '"What's this? Am I falling? My legs are giving way…' Above him there was now nothing but the sky—the lofty sky, not clear yet still immeasurably lofty, with grey clouds gliding slowly across it. 'How quiet, peaceful and solemn…How was it I did not see that lofty sky before? And how happy I am to have found it at last. Yes! All is vanity, all is falsehood, except that infinite sky. There is nothing, nothing but that. But even it does not exist, there is nothing but quiet and peace…'" That was how it was, for me, in those moments—those moments when I knew for sure my life was coming to its end. Things opened up for me; the world opened. I could not truly see until I had lost myself.'

Some days later, this conversation still vivid in my thoughts, I drove on, down the southern road, which I hardly knew: the track that leads through deep gorge country, past Baker Lake and the Yapuparra outstation turn-off, beneath a flat-topped hill seen, and named, by the explorer Frank Henry Hann in 1903 on one of his periodic, despairing thrusts across the sand dunes. Up ahead of me, at a bend, beside a dry creek line, in the shade of a large bloodwood, was a white Land Cruiser, parked, its doors open. The driver was kneeling in front of the bloodwood's trunk, notebook in hand. I slowed. He made a sign to stop. I recognised him: he was one of the old doctors from the travelling health-service team.

'Wonderful, isn't it?' he called out. 'Don't you think? The contrast: between this, this immensity'—he spread his hands, and gestured vaguely westwards—'and this. The precision of it, the humility.'

There was a blaze on the tree, and a metallic sign.

'It's a survey mark,' I said.

'Not at all. It's a Beadell plaque! It's almost a religious object.'

We introduced ourselves. He gave me an appraising look.

'You do know the story, don't you?' he said. 'About the Beadell roads, and Len Beadell, and the kind of man he was? How he came out into the deserts, with his Gunbarrel Construction Crew, in the fifties, and made every highway and every track we drive on today. He's a figure of great importance to me: in fact, I'm retracing his steps, and checking all of his co-ordinates and descriptions. I'd like the road network he built to be listed on the heritage register some day.'

'You want the roads to be preserved and protected? So no one would be able to drive on them?'

'Absolutely—although of course it would be impractical, from some points of view. At any rate, we can pay tribute to Beadell: I'm making plaques of my own, to record my own recording. Here—have a look!'

He held out a little square of aluminium, stamped with figures and letters, for my inspection—'Connie Sue Highway inspection survey...' I began to read the words out loud; but the plaque glinted in the sun, and dazzled me. I formed a picture in my mind of a dystopian future, in which every tree and every rock and prominence in the desert or the remote inland has a metal plate affixed to it, recording the visit of some exploration or re-enactment party traipsing through the bush—and indeed that vision will soon be well on the way to fulfilment, if the trends of recent years are prolonged, and the need our species feels to mark and emblazon nature continues to express itself.

'And have you spent much time on the Gunbarrel roads?' asked the doctor.

'A reasonable amount,' I said. 'In fact, now you bring it up, I imagine I've probably spent more time in the company of Len Beadell, in recent years, than any other human being—at least if you consider him still to be present in some sense, along the roads he worked on.'

'So he's almost your closest companion, then! And what brought you to devote yourself to deserts: what lures you out to where there's nothing, and it's all around?'

I laughed, at this. I felt both distant from myself and close to my inmost thoughts: they seemed to hang displayed before me in precise order, like an illuminated spider's web.

'And what if I were to tell you the truth?' I said. 'Or something like it, on the principle that truth is reserved for those people in life you're sure never to meet again?'

'Why not?' he said, encouragingly.

I thought back: I reached down, into old memories, and told him something of the days when I was growing up, in foreign countries, and how I used to haunt the cinema, wherever I found myself; how the cinema seemed much more ordered than the world outside; how even then I noticed that there were films that lasted a long time in the mind, and I could see the image winning out against the word. I went into detail: the flavour of that time, the way it had seemed, the way it looked in retrospect. I began telling him about the particular film-maker whose work most caught me up, and drew me on.

'He was Russian,' I said. 'And when I started travelling in remote country, and had no bearings, I found I remembered him: the way he valued each object, each living creature, each component of the visual field for its own sake. There was no hierarchy—and that seemed a crucial clue for out here.'

'You mean he taught you to look—to see on the desert's own terms?'

'That was his lesson, in a sense. The great film he made was a fiasco—but it had a splendour to it. It was a nature study, only it was a study of the way things are in a new world: a special zone, formed after a nuclear disaster, a place where everything is wrecked and desolate, and there's nothing easy for the heart or for the eye to take, yet there's still the presence and the pulse of life—and life's faintest trace is always the most beautiful; the harshest landscape is the loveliest. Just like the bleak, white salt lakes on this road, or the bare claypans, or some burnt patch of spinifex—you scrape down, you find insects moving, you look about, you see the spores of lichen; you stay quiet, and soon enough there's some hawk that flies over you, or some scatter of painted finches hanging round.'

'Very metaphorical!'

'It gets more so. The idea, in the film's story, was that in that zone, there was a single, hidden room, amid all the rubble and the radiation—a room where you could find your heart's desire—and as the years go on, and I look back, it occurs to me that the desert—the whole desert—is something very like that secret room, where your inmost wishes, which you can't even recognise yourself, come true.'

'How strange,' he said, then. 'How coincidental! And perhaps I should tell you, more truthfully, what brought me down this trail.'

He settled back: I sat down beside him, and leaned against the bark of the bloodwood tree. I shielded my eyes: the sun beat down.

'Time covers things so fast,' he went on, softly. 'So fast! History comes and goes. You probably don't even realise there were nuclear explosions here, in the desert, half a century ago—or if you do, I dare say you know next to nothing about them: the way they were planned, then carried out; the achievements, the mistakes. Maybe you've heard of Yami Lester—the blind man, who became well known, and who spoke at the hand-back of Ayers Rock. When he was a young boy, living with his family in the bush, they were downwind of one of those tests, at the Emu Junction site. You can go there today: it's not hard to reach. It's in the Woomera restricted zone. There's a little concrete pillar, quite elegant in its design. It says, "Totem II—A British atomic weapon was test exploded here on 27 October 1953", but it doesn't give much detail about what happened then: about the black mist that sprang up from the surface of the sand, and rolled up from the south, and enveloped Yami and all his family, and spread further still, and left desolation in its wake.

'I was a child then myself, far away, in the south. When I became a doctor, and I was doing my training in Adelaide, I was extremely idealistic. I had the grandest ideas about helping people, preserving life. I decided to specialise in nuclear medicine: radiation treatment. That was the time when the McClelland Royal Commission began conducting its hearings into the effects of the Maralinga tests. It was my field: they asked me to take part. I listened to the testimony. Beadell was there, giving evidence: that's when I first crossed his tracks. And I think it was a necessary kind of relief for me, to become interested in his journey, in that way there always has to be someone, up in front, just as you said, to lead you on.

'Beadell hadn't paid too much attention to the tests and what happened afterwards: that was clear. It was all an adventure for him, like everything out bush, really, for people in those days. But I knew: I knew, when I was sitting in the hearings of the commission, what the shape of the rest of my life was going to be. I knew I was going to spend it travelling between desert camps and run-down outstations, between old, dying men and women, watching them fade away.'

He broke off. He turned to me.

'And do you think death is the end of the line? I have to ask.'

'That's quite a question,' I said. 'From a medical man!'

'When I was studying,' he then said, 'and learning about the body and its intricacies, I almost believed we couldn't die. There would be no point to such a thing of beauty, such a wondrous mechanism, if it was all to pass away, and come to dust. There would be no point. But coming out here made me change my mind. Once I took it for granted that we would survive mortality; that nothing collapses except the crude house of the body, and the spirit lives on, somehow— and even when that belief went, I still liked to think we were all one, and connected with everything around us: the plants, and trees, and rocks.'

'But now?'

'Now? You can see me as I am. No disguises out here. I travel the bush; I visit communities, and tend to their needs as best I can; and at every turn I see in my mind's eye that black mist, sweeping through the landscape, sweeping up every last thing that sustains us in this world.'

'So you drive out here to escape—into the emptiness?'

'Escape—and also confirm. It has a comic aspect, don't you think? We believe that we can master nature: but we are our own first victims. Nature has become the sign of sadness for us. How much we destroy just by being! It's too unbearable to look at for very long.'

While he had been speaking in this way, a low cloud base had formed on the horizon, and was approaching, at some speed, from the west. It had covered nearly half the sky already, and beneath it there was a blur, a shadow, elusive, in which coils and light shafts seemed to whirl. The wind began to pick up. The temperature dropped.

'Have you been noticing that formation,' I asked, 'over there?'

'Indeed I have,' he said. 'A sandstorm coming: quite a big one. Time to keep moving. The right end, really, I think: the perfect ending for our talk.'

# IV

# The Mirror That Creates

*Australia Imagined in Western Eyes*

In the green heart of Adelaide, near the centre of the lush Botanic Gardens, there stands a palazzo from the mid-nineteenth century, made of glass, German-designed, indeed German-manufactured, built in its component parts in the Hanseatic port city of Bremen and transported in this fragmented form all the way to the southern hemisphere. It was commissioned by the keen-eyed Moritz Richard Schomburgk, the curator of the new parklands, a systematic plant collector, a man of grand ambitions, who bore a strong resemblance in both looks and cast of mind to the composer Wagner, his near-exact coeval. Schomburgk's long apprenticeship in scientific gardening had been performed at Sanssouci, amid the palaces and glasshouses of Potsdam: he had travelled through the wilds of British Guinea on an expedition with his older brother Robert, a celebrated explorer, and written a three-volume account of their journey; and these experiences had convinced him that the equatorial palm trees he wished to import would not be able to withstand the chill of the South Australian climate— though palms, in fact, thrive across almost the entirety of the continent.

Hence the structure, part of Schomburgk's plan to transform the garden area from 'a sterile waste' into a realm of instructive beauty. The glasshouse is ornate, it is majestic, its lines soar upwards; and the eye follows them, at once seeing the sweep of the columns to the geometric cupola, and seeing through them to the clouds above and the blue of the sky. There were other such pavilion buildings in the great gardens and parks of Germanic Europe; there was one in Bremen until the Thousand-bomber Raids of World War II; but there was nothing else remotely like it in Australia—and the arrival of the palace in kit form and its assembly close by the winding channel of the Torrens river symbolised the grand destiny of Adelaide, and knowledge's spread through enlightenment around the globe.

Its story was well-enough known for me to have heard it told in my childhood, and when I first began visiting Adelaide I remember seeking it out. Those were strange journeys for me. The cityscape was unfamiliar. Its order and its clarity were new to me, but I felt I knew its look, or I had walked its avenues up and down and seen its long vistas before. Above all there were two landmarks that stood out for me—the General Post Office on the corner of King William Street and the lovely old Town Hall, both buildings with ornamental towers crowned by baroque cupolas, slender, clad in stone.

I turned this impression over in my mind for weeks on end, before I realised. Those towers shining in the air had summoned up a memory, a memory of a sight I had never seen, and I could not have ever seen: the façades and domes of Dresden, on the banks of the Elbe, deep in East Germany, a capital that was once the glory of the Saxon lands, and was reduced to rubble in the last days of the war in Europe—destroyed, disassembled so thoroughly that the early topographic paintings made of the city were the best and most enduring guide to what it once had been. They were painted by the Italian master Bellotto, and they have about them a disquieting precision—the precision of dreams. A number of these works are on view in the galleries of Central Europe. I had seen one of them: it made a strong impression on me. The stone bell of the Frauenkirche rising high above the eaves of all the buildings round it, the colonnades and terraces along the gleaming river—they became emblems of perfection in my mind, all the more perfect because they were gone.

It was these lost sights and views that Adelaide and its spires and stone façades were summoning up for me. A dizzying relay—one that lets me edge nearer to a subject that has long drawn me and filled my thoughts, and seems thrown into sharp relief by the descent lines and visual parallels I have just been tracing out: the precise nature of the relationship between Australian and European, or western, writing; the links between these cultures; the interplay of their traditions, one so long established it seems through-composed and complete in every detail, one still struggling to take on its true contours and its autonomy and settled shape.

Where is the glass transparent and where mirrored in the transmission system of ideas and word pictures that binds north and south? Which way do the influences flow in the glasshouse of literary and cultural design? I would like to explore these links from several angles: first by looking at the way Australia and its art, literature and systems of thought were established by outsiders, incomers, settlers using a language foreign to the landscape; then by turning briefly to a different process, more telling and intriguing, and much less well recognised—the part in the history of ideas played by this continent, and what was becoming known of it, and the things that knowledge set in mind; the way Australia and the hard lessons it has to teach helped bring about a gradual transformation in the world at large, helped change what had long been fixed and certain in the wider realms of thought.

And it is my intention to move towards this maze-like set of problems, and beyond, with light steps, slant-wise, stealthily, for no notion worthy of the name in art or culture can be caught properly unless one sneaks up on it, catches it unawares, ambushes it—and even then it is the way of such things to try to hide in plain view, surrounded by all their familiar camouflage of conventional thoughts and preconceptions, much in the way a kipara, a bush turkey in the far Western Desert, will stand stock-still, it head craning upwards to the heavens, its neck almost too slender for a bullet from a .303 to hit—there, but impossible for us to seize, defined by all its elusiveness, until we come to wonder: what stays and what goes in the play of models and ideas and influences, what is enduring, what picture survives and what is lost—and is what we hand down and transform the thing that most truly lasts?

*

The patterns run through time: the descent lines. They make their channels and entrench them—but how to read them in the glass? Of course Australia was built against the European mirror; this culture's space was shaped in great part by design, through words, in the minds of men and women—much as Adelaide was conceived by deliberate intent, and laid out with northern ideas and influences held in tension in its grid.

And though this constructed, fabricated aspect of Australia's nature is scarcely to the fore today in the great cities of the southeastern seaboard, it seems to me that one can still sense it in the remote bush and the far inland: one can look back there to the time when Australia was largely a project of the imagination, a story still to be written—the ranges and the river systems and the claypans were not imprinted with the dust of written records from long centuries gone by.

It is a simple thing to imagine that the great explorers and investigators have only just retreated from the country; their spirits still linger there; the landscape is alive with their ideas and with their presences, active, hanging just out of reach. We can picture them. What did they see there, and experience there? When they went out, they were struck by the contrast between the unmapped inland of those days and the world they had come from—Northern Europe, charted, divided by frontiers historical and political. That difference was itself the key; it was the spur to the efforts of the first surveyors, mineral hunters and scientific classifiers as they fanned out across the country from the frail coastal settlements. A gallery of dreamers and chancers, dragging their hopes and fears behind them, writing and recording their way through what seemed to them like emptiness, silence, formless space. These first views of Australia helped determine what it became. You can trace them down various family lines of thought.

There are the naturalists and botanisers, all descendants of Joseph Banks, the great architect of the colony of New South Wales, the father figure of antipodean scientific studies. It was he who dispatched the fiery-tempered Allan Cunningham to travel with Oxley into the bush, and with King around the coasts, as first investigator and collector, to be followed by scores of other eager scholars, Schomburgk among them, and Frederick Bailey, the dutiful plant collector of the Adelaide plains, until the culmination of the line in that classifying obsessive Baron Ferdinand von Mueller, the bearer of an obscure title from the royal house of Württemberg, the author of a flood of works, among them his majestic atlas of Australian gumtrees, or *Eucalyptographia*—but a field man so devoid of aptitude that on his sole expedition of significance, through the Victoria River District with Augustus Gregory, he was almost always on the verge of getting lost. He was a profuse correspondent in a mingled array of languages, a bitter foe of evolutionary theory, an individual so marooned in thought he allowed his underclothes to decay gently into his flesh over the seasons and decades, and thus built up a kind of matted cotton fabric embonpoint, quite noticeable in archival photos of the baron in his later years.

Such were the European men who found the flora and fauna of Australia, and gave currency to the notion of the southern continent as a different natural kingdom, a new blueprint, an alternative creation—and that idea, much like a containing, regulating glasshouse, a structure thrown round life, transparent, all-shaping, was critical for the thinkers and theory-builders of the colonial nineteenth century.

It was a persuasive idea, strengthened by the tales the first explorers of the deep inland returned with, and the more nuanced narratives they wrote: works quickened, lifted up by the tempestuous passions of the time. The explorers: George Grey, whose premature birth was triggered by news of his father's death on the battlefield at Badajoz; the drama-courting Edward Eyre; the vision-haunted Charles Sturt, that schoolfellow of Lord Byron; the Camões-translating, Sophocles-quoting Thomas Mitchell; Ludwig Leichhardt, the prince of long, implication-laden paragraphs—what were they but romantic travellers, restless, drifting spirits, unsure of what they believed in, pilgrims in a bushland without variation, seeking for the contours of their dreams.

Consider Grey, who served for four years in the 1840s as the governor of South Australia, and was the most brilliantly successful of those early, literary-minded explorers. He can offer us a glimpse of this sensibility, which coloured all the first reports from the far north and the remote inland, and conveyed to the wider world a forbidding picture—dunes, savannah, wilderness, revelations lurking out of reach. Hence one foundation image of the Outback, as hard, inhuman, featureless—a land to exploit, but not one to love. Grey was in his mid-twenties when he led a catastrophically ill-equipped expedition to the harshest corner of the continent, the far northwest, and the coastline of the Kimberley. He was the western discoverer of the Wandjina rock-art tradition. He likened the round, staring faces of the spirit figures he saw in caves and beneath red rock-platform overhangs to the haloed sun symbols one saw on signs before certain English public houses. He loved fine words, and romantic attitudes; he was a leader of heroic will and bravery. When speared and dangerously wounded by Aboriginal assailants, he kept his injury from his men for some while to keep them from becoming disheartened.

Here he is, travelling through ravines and scrub and sandy downs covered by banksia trees. His thoughts wander, as if to free him from the dreary wastes around him—'but the necessities of the moment would not permit me to indulge in these speculations, and we turned therefore from the seductive travels of the imagination to the more stringent ones of reality'—and it is only when one reads one's way through the early expedition narratives, and encounters passages of this kind repeatedly, that it becomes plain how much the discovery of Australia was a literary, a creative venture, with extremity and insight advancing hand in hand.

The images, the tropes, the ways of seeing: they were all imports. The explorers carried them in their saddlebags as they rode out towards the blue horizon line. The country was first laid down in their words, and that influence is still alive, most vividly in the penumbral tradition surrounding Leichhardt, the Prussian virtuoso of the inland, the mystery voyager: linguist, geologist, naturalist, navigator and ethnologue, a man whose fate defines his life. For those who know them, Leichhardt's letters are a novel of turbulent, suppressed desires. The journal he published of his successful expedition from Moreton Bay to Port Essington is a work of romance, a love song to the landscape, the curtain raiser for the continental crossing he embarked on in April 1848, when he set off from the settled districts of the Darling Downs with his seven companions, his packhorses and equipment, and vanished without trace—and this vanishing has itself done much to shape the image of the Outback. It has its echo in Patrick White's *Voss*, and a score of other fictions; and the quest to find the explorer's trail is still alive today, as if seeking, searching were somehow the heart of the Australian project, as if there are veils still to be lifted, secrets and meanings still to be found in the inland.

Two modern writers have felt Leichhardt's absence most strongly, and have made repeated explorations of their own over the course of their lives in the bush, in the attempt to uncover something of his traces. Dick Kimber, the raconteur and tale collector of Alice Springs, the lingerer by the post office on Hartley Street, first took Leichhardt into his thoughts decades ago, and began a quest in the dune fields of the Simpson Desert. And there were clues in abundance then to guide him on his way, for Kimber listened to Aboriginal testimony, much of it provided in fine detail, and several of the tales spun from those encounters find their echo in his literary masterpiece, *Man from Arltunga*, a book ostensibly devoted to the life of Walter Smith, the celebrated bushman of the Eastern Plenty—though it is in truth a brisk *Thousand and One Nights* of desert storytelling, a yarn cycle, a campfire narrative of the highest artistry.

How different is the Leichhardt tale of Darrell Lewis, in literary persona a lone wolf, a haunter of back tracks, well versed in the Victoria River region where the desert and savannah landscapes meet, for Lewis has come to believe the explorer and his men travelled along the northern margin of the arid zone, skirting the dunes and staying with the river channels, until they reached the Tanami, and Sturt's Creek, and beyond, even, by a tortuous series of meanders—twists and turns reminiscent of the path Lewis himself has followed in his writings, which range from a detailed study of broncoing techniques to surveys of Arnhem Land rock art and an evocation of the 'ghost road of the drovers', the Murranji Track that once ran through the Top End's thickest lancewood scrub. These are the latter-day inheritors of that first European tradition the explorers left—the picture of Australia drawn by incomers.

The most delicate feat of intellectual engineering fell, though, to the human scientists of colonial times, who had to make sense of the Australian Aborigines, and did so in narratives that configured the country anew, and set in stone racial concepts and categories that are still dominant. Once the exploration frontier had closed, and the cycle of resource exploitation had begun, administrative skills were required to delimit and restrict the movements and behaviour of the native population, and knowledge of their ways was needed, too, in order to inform those skills. This was the birth context for Australianist anthropology, a classifying system par excellence, which lingers on into our time, tormented by its past and vexed by the contradictions of its present.

It was outside eyes that defined Aboriginal culture; outsiders studied it, as they still do, in the most exorbitant and voyeuristic detail. Religious and social practices, beliefs and rituals, artistic productions, song cycles—all these were recorded and written up, and the resultant books were devoured with great enthusiasm by the savants of the wider world. The Aboriginal peoples of Australia occupied an unusual position in colonial history. They were the land's first inhabitants; they were redolent of it; they had imprinted themselves upon it. It was in them: as a result, there was a certain need for them to be pushed to the margins during the decades of settlement and consolidation, the Federation time, when Australia's institutions were being born; and there was an odd, low-key, regret-tinged relief when it became clear that the numbers of the remote population were declining, that there was even a possibility they might be dying out.

But the discovery created a double bind, and, eventually, an artful resolution. As they passed from the scene, it was crucial to record them, measure them, preserve the evidence. This salvage paradigm is at the heart of the extraordinary sequence of works of scientific survey and literary evocation that poured from the pens of Australia's great field researchers in those years, with Spencer and Gillen, that unlikely duo, to the fore.

Sir Walter Baldwin Spencer was Manchester-raised and Oxford-educated, an evolutionary biologist of international standing, an art collector, an institution-builder, a writer and lecturer of the utmost verve. Francis Gillen, the son of Irish migrants, began his working life as a messenger boy at Clare, and rose through the ranks to become the Outback postmaster of Alice Springs. It was there that the two met, during the course of the pioneering Horn scientific expedition to the centre. They understood each other; they shared a fascination for the tribal men and women whose camps they saw all round them. They wished to know that world. They began a collaboration that endured for decades; their account of native life became the standard version; and it was Spencer, the professor, the dignitary, whose name came first. Once again it was the metropolitan view that took priority: outside eyes determined what Australia, with all its riches and its puzzlements, was felt to be.

\*

Telling fragments; pieces from a consistent picture. The modern schema for the continent was established on a pattern, by incoming experts, in a range of linked disciplines and fields of thought. The more recent development of the country and its culture can easily, and convincingly, be cast as a separate, second phase, a struggle between imposed and home-grown views. Such was the constitutive background, the ground condition of the Australian settlement. Two stages. Creation, and reaction. This background is all-structuring and at the same time submerged beneath the surface of national life and thinking, unnoticed, a figure in the carpet's weave, a tint in the prevailing light—but it has profound effects.

The consequences of that first stage stay with us. The ideas and concepts that shaped Australia came from elsewhere; the words we use now to describe it, too. Our language is an import. It did not develop here organically. The English that we speak came with Arthur Phillip and his band of men and women. It is maladapted to the continent, and to the inland, though it is the universal language of our time, and it is simple, and full of utility, and, like every vernacular, it is in a state of rapid evolution; it is constantly being exchanged and remade on the waves of speech. But there is still a subtle gap between the words of our tongue and the country around us, the phenomena of nature, the sights and the sounds in the air, the animals and wildlife—and so scientific words and loan words from Aboriginal languages have flooded into our vocabulary and become part of our day-to-day conceptual equipment.

*

How clear this becomes if we make a brief foray beyond our confected and well-controlled urban surrounds, and penetrate into the interior, to the Flinders Ranges, for instance, and set off on a little journey, an exploration of our own—but wait: it's plain at once. They aren't really ranges, in the true sense of the word, so much as light crustal folds; they are gentle, not steep; they are discreet and unemphatic, not high and conventionally sublime; and why are they named for Flinders, a surveyor with no connection to that country? There are creeks there, but no water flows in them; they are flash-flood channels, nothing more. There are gumtrees lining them, but these are not trees that share the look or the life cycle of a European tree in the forest landscape of our language's distant past, when the associations of its words were laid down and the nets of their meanings were tied together. In that world, in those times, trees gave shade, and they bore fruit in season; they dropped their leaves in winter. A gumtree of the inland lives for fire; it seeds through fire; the shade its leaves cast is a memory of what shade might be, rather than the real thing. Its trunk is a repository for ants and termites; its roots are shallow; the soil it stands in is not the deep topsoil of a European field but a red, iron-oxide-stained substrate. There are lakes on the horizon; they gleam and glint; but they are salt, and the water that they seem to hold is nothing but a mirage.

The mismatch is slight, but palpable. The divide, the structuring gap between the deep-buried associations in the words we use and what we see before us, and apply those words to, is more than just a minor inconvenience in the language we have inherited, a difficulty we can steer past. It breeds something. It creates something: a space for the free play of the imagination, a mood, as well, a tonality, well-masked, a faint sense of being adrift which many writers in the Australian landscape manifest almost at a subterranean level of their thought. And this sets up a tension, for the very fabric of the language seems to look elsewhere, to scan some horizon. Hence a yearning, a nostalgia for a world that is not present, and cannot be present. Loss and longing are coded in. And with them comes an urgent quest for plenitude, for connection, a heightened focus, a skew in the world—and I often feel that I can hear this primordial whisper in the Australian memoirists and poets of the past century whose works mean the most to me.

I also suspect that this condition has multiple consequences today. It is always quietly announcing itself; it keeps open a certain self-consciousness in the culture. It has sparked an appetite for strongly place-based writing, and a counter impulse, a fierce receptivity to foreign literature. And it has helped create, in recent times, an enthusiasm for indigenous art and story: Aboriginal words and narratives are words and narratives bound to the land. If this lean, this inclination in the language affects those born into it in subtle ways, the disconnect has always been of a different and more immediate order for incomers travelling to Australia, moving through it, studying and taking in its newness, sinking themselves in its strange atmospherics. What they would encounter was a world that failed to fit: a challenge.

*

And here is my second theme, a kind of wild inflection of the first. Yes: the mental climate of the new settlement was the product of, was laid down through, imposed words and disciplines—but its nature struck through this screen. There was a blowback: knowledge, ideas and experiences flowed from the Australian periphery, and influenced the way the centre thought and felt. And the tokens of this can be detected very early. They begin with the young Charles Darwin, who arrived in New South Wales on 12 January 1836 at the end of the survey vessel HMS *Beagle*'s South American and Pacific cruisings. Almost at once he set off on a field trip inland, to the Blue Mountains and the country beyond. His ideas about the order of the world were shifting; he was all surmise and speculation; and there was a far-seeing, aerial quality about his thinking in those days which may well have been influenced by the lofty verse he steeped himself in during the course of his shipboard travels, Wordsworth, Coleridge and, above all, Milton—the Milton of *Paradise Lost*.

One evening, leaning against a sunny bank in the vicinity of the Coxs River, near Wallerawang homestead, Darwin fell to reflections on the 'strange character of the animals of this country', and those reflections had the free, unfocused flow of reverie. The creatures he saw before him called to mind the insects and the animals he had known in England. He set down in his journal the ideas that came to him. 'A disbeliever in everything beyond his own reason might exclaim: Surely two distinct creators must have been at work: their object however has been the same and certainly in each case the end is complete.' And Darwin's eyes then fell on the minute soil-trap engineered before him by an antlion. He inspected it. It was very like the trap a European antlion makes—but plainly the species was different. 'Would any two workmen ever hit on so beautiful, so simple and yet so artificial a contrivance? I cannot think so.' The distinct parallels between the different European and antipodean flora and fauna were clear to the eyes of a field naturalist: they were unmissable.

Darwin was advancing with swift steps towards his theory of adaptation. Animals were selected, somehow, by the processes of nature, selected to suit their environment. The grand outlines of evolutionary thinking hovered within his reach. Decades would pass before the theory was refined and perfected, decades of agonising and hesitating before Darwin was constrained to place his findings and his conclusions before the public, but the Australian example had sunk in, and changed his picture of the world.

And so it went, in myriad cases, in various fields of investigation during the years when Australia was being discovered by western eyes. So it went in geology, in mineralogy, in zoology and botany, in the study of the seas and ocean currents, the air and skies and stars—and it would be a fascinating project if a synoptic survey of Australia's impact on the world of early modern science could be written. It would be the story of an upheaval, an unexpected revolution: on a wide front evidence and empirical method were used to overthrow the primacy of established theories and ideas.

Nowhere was this shift in understanding more pronounced than in that most contentious field of study, the science of man. Vast palaces of theory had been swiftly raised up in the late nineteenth century, in tandem with the decline of western religion: theories of social order, of the mind and its development. And suddenly there was a rich quarry of unknown data to mine. Aboriginal evidence gave investigators and philosophic speculators new grounds for hope that they might at last discover the essence of the human species, undisguised by the distracting accretions of material culture. A golden age of research dawned, and it was also a golden age for a particular strain of Australian writing—the heroic anthropological narrative. If man was now the measure of all things, then study him: the pioneers set out into the bush.

Who could have imagined that Pallottine priests would pass years in the desert immersed in the fine grain of Kukatja metaphysics, or that a Hungarian psychoanalyst would descend on Hermannsburg mission, in the ranges west of Alice Springs, and devote himself to recording and interpreting the dreams of Arrernte children, and indeed develop a new model of cultural development on the basis of his research? Who would guess that a frontier surgeon with a special interest in philology might amass a collection of Aboriginal string figures in far western Queensland, or that a free-thinking feminist would travel to remote Cape York and find her life's great mission there, compiling detailed records of myth cycles and tracing the symbolism in decorated shields and ornaments? But so it proved.

Everything those field workers learned on the desert frontier and in the tropics, and everything they gathered up, their treasure troves of unfamiliar artefacts and sculptures—it all returned to the metropole, and circulated in the academies of London and in the European capitals. It dovetailed neatly with the artistic currents of the modern era. New ways of seeing were being brought to life, and new ways, too, of presenting what was seen: the broken images and picture planes of proto-Cubism Picasso furnaced from his encounter with African carvings and masks from the Torres Strait, the Parisian surrealism that exalted Aboriginal and Pacific artworks, the studied primitivism that enlivened the painting circles of pre-war Dresden and Berlin.

Let just one striking instance of this transmission stand for scores of others. You may think we are very far, right now, from the realms of the signifier, and structuralism, and the promiscuous children of that thought-current, deconstruction and cultural studies, in all their rich complexity—but you would be wrong. Ideas and evidence from Australian research filtered into the key foundation text of modern structural anthropology, the first encyclopaedic work of Claude Lévi-Strauss, *The Elementary Structures of Kinship*—a book that traced the laws of social organisation to the incest taboo, and made use of detailed examples from Arnhem Land.

The marriage rules were so complex that Lévi-Strauss had to turn to his mathematician colleague André Weil, brother of Simone, to sketch the combinatorics for him. They appear in an appendix, and it is a diverting thing to wonder just how precisely this frantic binarism, this division of the entire cosmos into two opposed yet supporting categories, rhymed with a deep-seated strain in western religious thinking, the Gnostic strain, which found its echo in Judaic Kabbalism, and was surely a submerged current in the first foundations of French ethnography, as pioneered by Émile Durkheim, a man of strict rabbinic background, and passed on to his nephew Marcel Mauss, and taken up in turn by the next in the descent line at the Musée de l'Homme, Lévi-Strauss; and equally the mind lingers on the sharp effect of this double-structure model on the subjects of the field investigations that lent it air and life. It was the young American anthropologist Lloyd Warner who brought the moiety kinship system of the Yolngu of North

East Arnhem Land to wider view, and often nowadays one encounters doctoral students dragooning their informants in the communities and outstations of the Top End, until, in keeping with the dogmas of the established theory, they have successfully divided up every single component of the natural and sensory world into two elegantly balanced camps.

*

And so, from such antipodean clues in a range of fields of study, a newly accented picture of mankind could take form: one that saw the subtlety and depth in nomadic societies; one that overturned the old paradigm of cultural evolution, in which social groups developed in slow advance, from the primitive condition of hunter-gatherers, through settled agriculture, until they could reach their natural endpoint, and become like the grand civilisations of the European West.

But the West, by then, was in ruins—the dark twentieth century had begun, the time that changed the balance of the world and its parts entirely. It changed the place and meaning of the Australian continent, as well. In the years before Federation, Australia was still subsidiary, a colonised space, with ideas and thought-grids imposed upon it, a colonial administrative and economic pattern, and a stamp of derivativeness about much in its approved and publicly disseminated culture. Then came the cascade of disasters of the mid-century, disasters for Britain, and for the coherence of Europe: the Great War, the Depression, and the second, German war, which divided and distorted the whole West for half a century until the Berlin Wall came down.

It was an age for seeking open horizons, new sights and thoughts to replace what was soured, broken, overthrown—and almost as soon as the first, Great war was done a flow of experimental artistic and literary travellers spread out across the world, and my final focus is on this tide of incomers. What did they see and find in the Australian landscape? What did it give them, and what did they give back to it, and us?

※

D. H. Lawrence was in flight from Britain, on a 'savage pilgrimage', when he arrived in Australia in May 1922, took up residence for a brief period in the New South Wales coastal settlement of Thirroul, cloistered himself there in a bungalow, and in just forty-three days of writing poured out his novel *Kangaroo*, one of the most unusual masterpieces of the time, a work almost entirely generated by intuitions and half-suspected gleanings, a work much concerned with conspiratorial currents in Australian right-wing politics, and a book generally viewed with scant enthusiasm by readers and critical appraisers here.

Lawrence, doubtless, was searching for a landscape devoid of the clotting taint of Christian religiosity, for country he could see on its own terms, free from western history's distorting weight—indeed, the most startling feature of *Kangaroo* is its writer's receptivity to the landscape: Lawrence was the first well-known author of great gifts to describe Australia, to turn his eyes on the country, to tune his mind and heart to what lay around him. The chief advocate and defender of *Kangaroo* over the past generation, Simon Leys, catches the processes active in the pages of the book. Lawrence had taken into himself the mood of the country. He also sensed a deeper current running through Australia's brief settled history: 'Throughout the entire Nineteenth Century, the reactions of Anglo-Saxon visitors and settlers to the Australian landscape betray a deep uneasiness, even a sort of unspeakable fear.' So Leys, in his overview, and again:

> The early European pioneers were bravely determined to tackle nature, but their challenge fell flat; it merely encountered a colossal indifference on which all their energy could not find any grip...The inexpressible horror that was felt by the first settlers was rooted in one deep intuition: this is a world of such radical strangeness that it makes man lose all relevance—here man is completely superfluous.

But, for Lawrence, it was precisely the strangeness and the lack of context that was appealing, and the land had different accents. The flower blueness of the air, the foliage, the brown of the low rocks, the frail inconspicuousness of the landscape—all these seemed striking and beautiful to him, even though he knew very well that for the Australians he came into contact with during his stay such features were simply the unvarying carpet of the country, monotonous, devoid of associations, a vista they failed to see. Lawrence not only saw it. He saw something beyond, or behind, the landscape as well—something else.

> It was virgin bush, and was as if unvisited, lost, sombre, with plenty of space, yet spreading grey for miles and miles, in a hollow towards the west. Far in the West, the sky having suddenly cleared, they saw the magical range of the Blue Mountains. And all this hoary space of bush between. The strange, as it were invisible beauty of Australia, which is undeniably there, but which seems to lurk just beyond the range of our white vision.

\*

Plainly the ensuing decades have been corrective ones, as if the course Lawrence charted could be followed easily once laid out, as if the turn in sensibility was already on. Time, changes in patterns of thought and reflection, the growth of a landscape nationalism, the taking of a distance from old-world models of sublimity: all these have played their part. Attitudes to the country and to its physical presence are different. The stretch of bush Lawrence was describing, inland from Thirroul and the Illawarra, is one of the most admired and cosseted and tended stretches of bushland in the world today.

But the case is instructive. Why such an impact on Lawrence? Why does he, after a few months spent in southern Australia, stand as the first writer of true significance to catch the country: long before Patrick White, long before Randolph Stow. We are confronted by the mysterious capacity of incomers to see—and I believe it is not just a story of particular genius, or acuity of vision. Nor is it only a question of fresh eyes, unprepared by images of the new continent, and of a mind like Lawrence's, lost in idea creation, devoted to explorations and probes in language, to finding new nets of sights and textures to describe. No: it is the wider scene.

I wrote earlier of the West in ruins, north Europe in ruins, and this was nothing figural. In the mid-twentieth century its lovely buildings and cathedrals stood pulverised; its artistic landscape was torn by conflicting currents; it was a shattered moral and intellectual space.

How, after this, to believe in man's order, and in his religion? How to live when the centre has not been able to hold? It is hard now to give a succinct picture of the distress and anomie that gripped the high culture of European nations in the interwar years, and the post-war, and I had long despaired of doing so—until I came recently upon a brief passage in the first volume of the correspondence of Samuel Beckett, who, before he was a man of wordlessness and stage stillness, was a scholar, a translator, a creature of the highest literary formation; the secretary to James Joyce; the author, when only twenty, of a masterful study of Proust; a crown prince, in fact, of European letters. In mid-1937, with the Spanish Civil War filling the headlines, he drafted a note in German to the publisher Axel Kaun, refusing a commission. It has become well known, from Beckett's carbon, though he may not in fact have sent it. He sets out his dissatisfaction with his own language, English. More and more it seems to him like a word-veil one has to rend apart in order to reach the things—or the nothingness—lying behind it. It is a mask: it must be torn off, dismantled, drilled into until something starts to come through. The German original has quite a kick. Here is one key passage, translated, in which Beckett pleads for writing to be freed from the old straitjacket of rules and conventions, and the tyranny of style:

> Or is literature alone to be left behind on that old, foul road long ago abandoned by music and painting? Is there something paralysingly sacred contained within the unnature of the

word that does not belong to the elements of the other arts? Is there any reason why that terrifyingly arbitrary materiality of the word surface should not be dissolved, as for example the sound surface of Beethoven's Seventh Symphony is devoured by huge black pauses, so that for pages on end we cannot perceive it as other than a dizzying path of sounds connecting unfathomable chasms of silence? An answer is requested.

'I know there are people,' he continues, 'sensitive and intelligent people for whom there is no lack of silence. I cannot help but assume that they are hard of hearing. For in the forest of symbols that are no symbols, the birds of interpretation, that is no interpretation, are never silent.'

In its despair and anger and frustration, and its no-exit, end-of-the-line quality, its consciousness of played-out languages and decayed, half-rotted, near-fragmented cultural forms, this note—so fierce, so dashed-off—serves as a perfect X-ray of a world on the brink, and the sequel is familiar. But what this passage and everything it sums up hints at in the broader story I have been tracing out is the impact Australian sights and landscapes could have on European incomers in those years and decades when all seemed lost. The new land served not just as haven, as refuge. The country had, and still has, another role—it seemed to them to be a country without an overhang of failure, without a shattered past, without traditions fading into oblivion. It was a canvas without obvious marks on it. Old conventions held no sway. More than this, it was radically unfamiliar. It was able to disorient, it withdrew itself from the first glance of the eye, it suggested new forms, it forced new thoughts into the mind—and it played this role repeatedly in the mid-century's unfolding course.

*

This was what it did for Lawrence, who was in midlife when he arrived in Australia, his great novels already behind him, his haunted masterpieces of travel writing still ahead, works that, for many of his admirers, paved the way for new modes of speculative, open-ended narrative—fragments written from experience, but far from descriptive of the surface patterns of a life. Australia sharpened Lawrence's eye. It allowed him to focus on those features of the bush landscape that are most present and most resistant to our words: the landscape that begins to feature prominently in the art of the mid-century, and in more recent Australian literature, so strikingly that it becomes the main protagonist in the books of a range of writers, Eric Rolls and Les Murray to the fore.

The country also performed this kind of service for another, later incomer, another writer of international reputation who also saw something here unnoticed in plain view: Bruce Chatwin. It is very tempting for Australian observers to mock him, this pure exotic, who lacked the genius and consistency of Lawrence, and is within reach still of the long resentments of living memory, and got much of what he heard and saw creatively wrong, and was in essence a stylish travelling publicist—but the facts are plain. Chatwin arrived in Australia in 1983, and made quick visits to the centre and Alice Springs, and in much the same mysterious way as Lawrence he was able to grasp through intuition what no other imaginative writers of the time had quite managed to discover and return with—the grandeur, the sombre splendour of desert Aboriginal culture, its depth and scale. From the book he published on the basis of his journeys, *The Songlines*, inchoate and maladroit as it is, a whole cascade of Australian writing and thinking over the past generation descends.

Again, here is the phenomenon of the incomer lifted up, exalted by what those around him seem to take for granted. Chatwin wrote to his wife soon after his arrival in Australia, in a state of high enthusiasm:

> You've no idea how beautiful the land is, and the climate, just on the fringe of the arid and wet zones...Of course on one level, it's complete Cloud-cuckoo-land, really very far away from the rest of the world; and it's going through a

recession; but if anywhere has an underlying optimism this is it.

Again, there is in his case the capacity of the outsider to think things that hover almost beyond the range of the local writerly elite, or beyond the scope of what they are prepared to say. Chatwin was the ultimate jaded connoisseur of used-up Europe, the traveller in search of some new language. Above all he wanted a fresh kind of silence, not the overloaded silence of the funerary smoke draped over the old continent. He was in rebellion against standard, sequential forms of narrative; his instincts pushed him towards a landscape that lent itself to portrayal in fragments, in rhymes and patterns and reduplications. There was a current he could sense in Australia at the time he arrived. He aimed to catch it, and what mattered was as much the proclamation of his discovery as his excavation of its finer details in analysis of any depth.

These two examples make a striking pattern, little highlighted in the standard accounts of Australian literature and its progress, as if they were not a real part of its story—and I could expand my thesis for you with the tales of other incomers. I know very well that I have leapt and jumped from rock to rock in the flowing stream of words, and offered you something more like a high-speed literary car chase than a settled piece of history—but nevertheless I feel there is something here, in the priority of these two visitors, these drifting, self-exiled travellers, Europe's flotsam, figures who gave permission to Australian writers to see and frame what lay before their eyes. We have a sense of what they wanted, what they were seeking. What they found is quite another matter.

*

I have led you far: from my first image of the German glasshouse glinting in the hard southern sun, and my sketch of Australia's foundation in the western mirror, by outsiders, speaking foreign words, and my second theme, a counter-current of Australian knowledge flooding through the thought-world of the West. And now we are engaged with ways of seeing, ways of writing. It is all the same reflection, and I should like to close it with a pair of intuitions—about words, and breath.

This tale of outsiders coming in, and laying patterns down, and seeing first, and writing first, is not necessarily a bleak one of literary subsidiarity, or secondariness, or failure. For all the prominence of Lawrence and Chatwin, and the long sequence of gifted travellers of their kind, I suspect that they were simply sensing what was known, and felt, and even set down by earlier writers—but not so succinctly presented or so keenly advertised. I could find examples throughout the obscure archipelago of books and diaristic accounts and pamphlets penned in the early phases of colonial Australia:

histories, ethnographies, journey narratives. I could find you jewels well disguised, treasures almost hidden from the wider world, work by writers who withdrew themselves. And I tend to feel this reticence is linked to a falter in the language, the falter at its heart, the wound that must always be overcome: that break between expression and country which produces the tact and understatement in the old Australian culture's way with words, both written and on the tongue. This primal reticence seems to me to be the chief consequence of the first condition of Australia: the more one sees, the more one has a feeling one should fall silent, or say little—and I feel this pressure more and more, the longer that I spend in the remote landscapes of the centre and the north. I feel it pressing down.

*

All this has become much clearer to me in recent years. There was a time when I had come back to Australia after prolonged absence. I was travelling extensively then, through the Pilbara and the desert inland, acting on the idea that such journeys might reacquaint me with the country. And so it proved, but I found it hard to form the right words for what I was seeing, and for the sense I had of rhythm and pattern and light in the landscape, pattern that implied an eye to see it, but that held itself apart.

It was only some years later, when I made a long research trip to the remote north of the former Soviet Union, that these impressions came into a kind of belated focus for me. I had been there before, on closely guided visits in late communist times, to the great industrial cities of Siberia and Kazakhstan. I had seen something then of that landscape's emptiness and scale. I went back, for three reasons: to travel there alone; to be where writers who had meant very much to me, like Shalamov and Solzhenitsyn, had spent their hardest years; and to see something of the Gulag's fast-vanishing remains, and the old monastic settlements, and the lakes and the taiga, unending stretches of larch and spruce and pine tree, great forests reaching to the horizon's line. And it was a surprising thing to discover how similar that country was to the Australian inland: a mesmerising monotony, species of the same kind as far as the eye could see—harsh, unvarying, almost untouched by human hand.

There, in that frozen country, many of the lessons of the desert seemed clear, and to sense them in two different places made them clearer still. What was the taiga saying, and the desert country? The things Leichhardt heard, it may be, and Lawrence, perhaps, in his fashion, too. That man is not the measure of the landscape, and knowledge not the sole aim of our endeavours. What is the bush for us? It is so poor in its sights and sounds it is a wealth. It gives so little it sets you free. It tests you against yourself but takes your self away. What is the inland; what secrets does it hold for us?

You cannot live there, and survive there, without reverence: reverence for what is above you, reverence for what is on the same level as you, reverence for what is below you. On the wind, you can hear its words. It murmurs, it whispers to you. It says: You came into this world, which has no need of you, and you must strive here to complete yourself, to find the truth, find form in formlessness, find what is hidden from you in this blinding light.

*

A very European reflection, doubtless: very metaphysical! But we are in terrain that still bears a little of the impress of Europe and its traditions, and there may be no distinction to preserve between the two worlds for us in the end. I come back to the parklands in tranquil Adelaide, and the glasshouse, the transparent palace where our tale of influences began.

It was designed by Gustavus Runge, of Bremen, an architect once well regarded in his own country, though his surviving masterworks are all overseas. He spent some years in America, and there entered into partnership with Napoleon LeBrun. Together they designed the Philadelphia Academy of Music, a chandeliered and multi-tiered extravaganza. After a decade Runge returned to Bremen, and completed a number of eclectic structures there—mausoleums, castles, town residences—in Tudor Gothic, Neo-Renaissance and

Romanesque. He made a specialty of glasshouses, built on supports of slender metal, high in their reach, grand in scale, but of them all only the palazzo in Adelaide is still extant, a fact that explains the constant flow of architectural historians and academic specialists from north Germany who make pilgrimages to inspect the details of its design.

And perhaps a couple of them chance to look up, and notice the geometric cupola—octagonal—a reminiscence of the eight-sided cathedral dome of Aachen, the resting place of Charlemagne, the home church of the Holy Roman Empire, which had ceased to be some thirty years before Adelaide was born. There it is, the light of southern skies glaring through it—the emblem of all Europe's ancient grace and glory, transported halfway round the world.

# V

# What Lies Beyond Us

What is the secret that hides behind the landscape? What are the half-glimpsed shadow lines that draw us in? What mystery of energy or presence is it that we feel around us when we find ourselves alone in the bush, surrounded by the unfolding expanse of the country: plants, earth, ranges, sky, each element shaping and defining all the others?

These interlinked questions stand in close relationship to a different dilemma, a dilemma of a political, or moral, nature—one that faces us with ever greater clarity as each fresh year in the settlement of Australia grinds on. How should we conceive of our place in the landscape of the continent we have claimed as our own? Are we its custodians, masters, brokers, servants—and what is its place in our world of thought?

*

These issues only began to take form and gain prominence in my mind once I began travelling extensively on my own in the inland, and reading my way through the literature of the Australian landscape—the story of its exploration and discovery by westerners, of its ecology, of its nurture and its exploitation and gradual redesign at the hands of man. And as I look back now on those years of journeyings, when I used to think nothing of driving for weeks on end through the Kimberley or Pilbara, or the far Western Desert, down tracks I would fear to take today, I come to see that this was the phase of midlife for me, a time of recalibration, when received ideas fragment and one begins to take a surer grasp of the world. The things that have true resonance in one's being come to the fore; one sees again the sights of childhood; memory returns, and clears the way to further knowledge; one sees that frail darting swallow the self for what it is, a brief positioning of forces, a trace in time; one sees beyond what schooling first gave one to see of the world.

It was also in those days that I first encountered the books of Australia's foremost writer of landscape history, Eric Rolls. I remember the moment. I was in the somewhat jumbled, oddly organised bookshop of the State Library of New South Wales; it was a Saturday afternoon; I was browsing aimlessly; and in one of the bargain bins beside the front entrance, amid piles of genealogical studies and obscure monographs on public policy, I chanced upon a book titled *A Million Wild Acres*. There was a subtitle as well: *Two Hundred Years of Man and an Australian Forest*—and there was just enough of a hint of eccentricity about that phrasing to make me pick the book up. On the cover was a faded little rosette in cornflower yellow, of the kind publishers once used to favour: '*Age* Book of the Year 1981', it announced.

Who could resist? I plunged in, and I feel I have never quite escaped from those extraordinary pages, with their evocation of the history of the Pilliga Scrub, its creatures and its people. *A Million Wild Acres* opened a door for me. It described the bush in fine-grained detail; it found the beauty in its light and heat; it anatomised the wildlife of the scrub; it unravelled the pattern of the forest's growth and change. The cries of owls, the crack of seed pods bursting, the drift of pollen clouds through the branches, bees humming, cicadas calling, streams rushing, engines growling, old corrugated-iron shacks creaking—what did it not summon up? The bush was no longer a wilderness without distinction; it was full of grace and subtlety and depth.

Swiftly I pursued the author through his multiplicit backlist, becoming, in the process, more familiar than I had been with the art and science of cookery, the history of Chinese communities in Australia, algal blooms on the Darling River, and myriad other sub-disciplines, until at last I tracked down a copy of his first prose masterpiece, the vanishingly unfindable *They All Ran Wild: The Story of Pests on the Land in Australia*. It is a set of bravura essays detailing the spread and control of creatures as varied as foxes, rabbits, rats and dingoes. Its style is laconic, its field of evidence encyclopaedic, its touch light and perfect. On reading through its pages I had the uncanny feeling that I knew their writer, that I was in some diagonal fashion close to him.

A few years later I did in fact meet Rolls, and spend time in his company, and he proved to be the epitome of warm and generous charm; but of course, like all writers of stature, he lived for his work, there was a reserve about him, he kept the best of himself for it, he was caught up in it, and it was through his books that one could come to understand his way of placing himself in the flow of memory and time. Those books embodied a cast of mind, a manner of thought, but also a way of life, a tradition, a history set within the landscape—and it was that aspect of *A Million Wild Acres* that compelled the poet Les Murray to explore the book in a long critical essay every bit as rich and free-ranging and judgemental as the writing of Eric Rolls himself.

\*

This essay was first published in late 1982, a leisurely twelve months after the book it purports to review, but Murray's 'Eric Rolls and the Golden Disobedience' has such a quality of dash and freedom that it remains to this day a vital manifesto, setting out the special place of landscape literature in Australia, explaining the novel features of the enterprise and hinting at its overarching scale. Many of its assessments and its irresistible side-path meanders echo the ideas that swept through me when I was first making my way through *A Million Wild Acres*—and they clear the pathway to a wide plateau of thought and reflective artistry.

How best to survey it? I begin with the story of an evolution. The role of landscape and the bush in the Australian imagination has changed in telling fashion over the past three decades, and that shift can be traced through a handful of litmus works—but I have the sense that there is still further to travel down this road, and that forms of writing attuned to the landscape, in rhythm with country and with the realm of nature hold out the promise for us of a strange, late-dawning redemption, of rescue from the disquiet and near despair that fence in and threaten the enterprise of literature today. What is the horizon line that most fittingly draws us, that we should strive to reach? There are scores of enticing avenues of history and culture to follow up, but in the end they are just the easy, marked, blazed paths. The wordless questions the bush poses to us: they remain. This will be my endpoint: the still point where we must see with an inner eye.

Perhaps close observation and keen listening can be a first guide for us: looking and listening like Rolls, whose even, on-running descriptions sound exactly like the flow of casual talk, of campfire yarning, and yet conceal the utmost craft and compositional restraint. Here he is, in a glorious passage from *A Million Wild Acres*, which I singled out many years ago when I was seeking to set down some ideas about the Australian mode of writing, and which I later found Murray had himself selected as the climactic point of the narrative in his own account. It is the story of the great Pilliga bushfire of 1951, or an episode in it, presented in a sequence, rapid, the emotions of both writer and reader jumping here and there as the scenes flash by:

> Initially some of the firefighters were not worth feeding. With so little equipment they saw no point in risking their lives for a bit of scrub. They played cards and let it burn. A young sleeper cutter, not mentally normal, could not resist lighting a few extra fires. Others risked their lives trying to cut breaks with the little graders. Noel Worland worked the first 63 hours without sleep. Ned Edwards spent 13 days and nights at the fire, his brother, Roy, 18.
>
> Arthur Ruttley was sent to take up the charge. He organised big bulldozers from

coastal forests, five new graders from Sydney, water tankers from the RAAF. He flew in a plane load of forestry students to get experience. He recruited local volunteers and enough cooks to feed several hundred men. He kept everybody working. They put out the fire in three weeks.

Noel Worland watched the forests for further outbreaks from a De Soutter aeroplane flown by Dick Burt of Baradine. The high wings were made of plywood and they drummed as the plane came in to land. The noise got louder and louder till at touchdown it seemed the plane must disintegrate. Dick Burt's cattle dog rode with Noel on the back seat and licked his face while he was spotting. Each time he pushed it away it growled venomously.

An even piece of narrative: a tale in which every actor has a name, and part. Les Murray, on reading this vast 'regional-ecological' tapestry of stories, this shaggy-dog tale with actual shaggy dogs, was struck, naturally enough, by its remarkable thesis about the scrubland country around the little township of Baradine, today no more than a scatter of shops and houses surrounded by lush forest, all thick cypress pine and ironbark and manna gum. This treed landscape, Rolls concluded, on the basis of his archival researches, but also from his own observations and deductions, was recent, and the product of western man's influence: it had been sandy, open parkland in the days of sole Aboriginal occupation, when fires were routinely set to cleanse the country.

This was a radical interpretation in 1981: it is the received wisdom among many environmental historians today. The process was straightforward enough. Settlers came in, and with them came new plants and grasses and animals; the great trees grew and cast their shadow across the country. Cattle, horses, rabbits, dogs—they were the chief agents of the transformation, but there was the human tide as well, settlers. 'Capable, adventurous, and extraordinarily adaptable, difficult, crude, vigorous, dishonest, selfish, violent. They differed only in the extent to which each of these qualities was developed. It is no use wishing they were different. To do so is to dispense with our culture.'

And this is precisely what Rolls, in all his writings, was at pains to avoid. He wished to know, to drag the record of the past out into the light, to understand the agents and the forces that made Australia. He wanted to paint the country, not just its people. This led him to his particular method, which receives its most majestic long-form exposition in *A Million Wild Acres*, and has been taken up by a subsequent generation of writers and scholastic thinkers who make the land and its place in our life their chief concern. One can trace a chronological sequence of events in the book; there are chapters; but, as Murray says of it, its logic is accretive, 'made up of strings of vivid, minute fact which often curl up in intricate knottings of digression'.

It is, in short, a reflection of the bush itself in all its reduplications, and its beginning everywhere and nowhere, its undelineated expansiveness. Man is not the measure of this country, or this narrative: he has no special prominence. Rather, there is a sequence of highlighted anecdotes, and tales, and vignettes from nature, and a constant jumping between passages, and all this achieves a break from sequential time, and entry to a space Murray characterises as 'a sort of enlarged spiritual present in which no life is suppressed'. It is, of course, a perspective that calls to mind indigenous modes of narrative from remoter parts of Australia, the story cycles of the Western Desert, the songs of Arnhem Land; and it raises the thought that attention to the Australian landscape itself dictates the best way of describing Australian experience.

Murray is tempted to push the notion further: 'It is even possible,' he suggests, 'that the novel, a form we have adopted from elsewhere, may not be the best or only form which extended prose fiction here requires.' This is an argument that has also tempted me, and has helped incline me to turn away from purely fictive prose narrative in setting down my own responses to remote Australia, and towards a writing system more hybrid, more shaped by joins and correspondences, more conscious of the breakdown in forms and patterns and order in the world than of their establishment.

There is another reason for my reluctance to tread the wide, well-worn road of bounded, narrative-shaped fiction. I believe forms in art have their time; they are at their strongest and most immediate when newly forged, and the story for them from that point on is one of increasing complexity and continual decline—and we are at the very end of the novel's baroque evolution; it is life's surface mirror in a million iterations; its fashions are arbitrary; it is powerless against the curtained void modernity has hung around our eyes.

*

This crisis of the form is matched by a crisis of function—one so profound that many of the great luminaries and masters of contemporary writing fear it may prove terminal; one so dark that few authors and critics are prepared to face it and hold it unflinchingly in their field of vision. Can it really be that the age of textual art is dying, that the high literary forms of the bourgeois age are passing from us in a last sputtering flare of intricate designs? Will mass culture extinguish literary writing, or confine it to some subsidised ghetto, or to the stunting cloisters of academe? Must we conclude that books no longer shape life to their own proportions, that poets are no longer the unacknowledged legislators of the world, that those who frequent libraries and bookshops are merely members of an antiquated, dwindling sect?

The phenomenon is unavoidably evident: there it is, blotting out all else from view, looming high above us like some wet-season cloud tower of stratocumulus over the coastline of the Top End. And what is the point of finesse, when all is demotic, of subtlety when all is blatant, of restraint and self-effacement when we live in a western Babylon of narcissism? These elements in our surrounds increase year by year, like some slowly growing atmospheric impurity; they change the composition of the world we must seek to know and describe: but they also shift the role of the writer, and the reader. They transform the scope of written, edited, published words; they make the task of literary witness yet more problematic. How to find and write truth, when truth is veiled by the illusions and passing fascinations of the time: how to hold meaning in through-written plots and tales, when we are drowned in meaninglessness? This is one fearful aspect of the trap: the world is no model.

But the trap is multiple, and cunningly designed, so cunningly it seems like one of mankind's great achievements: the destruction of high culture may be revealed to us one day as high culture's most outré and most fatal triumph, a terrifying, necessary end. Not only do books feel weightless: those who write them feel weightless. For many western writers, the belief in writing, the faith in writing's power has begun to ebb, and fade, in much the way the fading belief in oracles slowly killed the Olympian gods. The sad, proud joke of Central European dissidents under late-communist regimes a generation into the past still rings true, if with a changed resonance, today: 'With us, nothing is free, and everything matters. With you, everything is free, and nothing matters.'

And it is constraint and control that come to mind when we think these questions through. I found the clearest and most shocking formulation of the plight before us at the close of a detailed essay on the literature of dictatorship, written by the American short-story writer Deborah Eisenberg. It was a brief, succinct passage. It made me read it and reread it. It had the force of revelation for me. Her argument was simple: fiction's power was slackening, the strength of falsification was rising in the world; but this assault on fiction was paradoxical, it was no assault at all. The forces arrayed against it were 'more complex, more subtle and harder to trace than the distortions of an entrenched dictatorship, or for that matter of pure market capitalism'. The problem was the thin air of pure licence: 'Here in the West,' she wrote,

> fiction writers are welcome to be absolutely outspoken; maddeningly, no one much cares what we say—we pose no threat. Is it because our writing is not sufficiently forceful? Because

our potential readership has been trained to look elsewhere to gain an understanding— or misunderstanding—of their world, or has been, in the course of the single-minded cultivation of an army of consumers, ruthlessly undereducated? Because what contemporary writers perceive and say is in some fundamental way divorced from reality?

An agonised inquiry for a writer to make, and set down in print: 'It is as if fiction has largely come to be treated as a self-enclosed area,' she concludes, 'and judged by standards that have little to do with the living world beyond it.' It has, then, lost its potency and its capacity to convince; it is no longer taken for reality, nor does it reach through to another realm. Eisenberg closes her assessment with these lapidary words:

> Whatever we have to say is in danger of being transmuted, as soon as it hits the paper, into something trivial and inessential. Perhaps part of the problem is that not only have we not located the obstacles to our meaningful expression, we hardly discern that there are any.

That was written years ago. The crisis is still before us; it has only deepened. It is a crisis not just of fiction, but of the entire wide field of imaginative writing in a time that looks for satisfactions beyond the written, static, marmoreal word. It is a global crisis, and it is local, it is with us here— indeed its effects could well be especially potent in Australia, given the hardscrabble origins of the writing tradition in this country, a place that outsiders treat as a sub-domain of the English-language empire, its books seemingly legible by English speakers all round the world without any great effort, seemingly component parts of a global common culture. The writing life here is no more than two centuries old, more properly, perhaps, just over a single century, if we seek to highlight books written from the perspective of a particular Australian consciousness. A shallow time-depth, a dependent position in the Anglosphere of publishing, a certain democratic reluctance to exalt high-culture forms that have a sheen of exclusivity about them—ground conditions of this kind might plausibly be expected to shadow our literary life.

But I see another landscape. I see a seriousness among the writers and the readers who share in the idea of Australia as an uncompleted project, a great book even today being composed and revised and continuously redrafted all round us, a new achievement of mankind: flawed, born in the night of dispossession, inchoate, provisional, but still in its days of configuration and design. I see a culture that remains unplayed-out, conscious of what lies before it rather than the golden chapters of an impossibly vanished, all-dominating past it feels obliged to desecrate; conscious, too, of the indigenous realm that at once questions and underpins it. Above all, I see a special tradition without match elsewhere, a tradition of works made in the likeness of the landscape, work attentive to the country, its look, its feel, its reticence. This is a tradition that would embrace Eric Rolls and Les Murray, but it stretches back before them, to the romantic landscape pioneers of exploration literature, and they have descendants, too, writers of our day.

A school has formed. Unsurprisingly, given the need to recover lost chapters of the history of Australia's settlement, it has a historical lean, but it is first of all a school of writing, caught up in the idea of place, in the idea of the Australian bush and ways of charting it, knowing it, matching it in words. The origins of this school may lie in the cultural nationalism of the mid-1970s, but it has earlier antecedents: the first local chronicle of Geoffrey Blainey, for instance, who was at pains to forge a fluent, supple kind of vernacular to convey the experiences of the miners of Mt Lyell in Tasmania's rugged west, or the diaries and journey memoirs set down by the mid-century scientist writers of the inland: Cecil Madigan, who crossed the Simpson, for one; and the biologists Elliot Lovegood Grant Watson and Francis Ratcliffe, who both felt impelled to seek a poetic comprehension of the country they researched. There is George Seddon, whose hybrid essays opened up the Pilbara for me when I was a student of the deserts; John Mulvaney, who made the history of encounters between westerners and indigenous Australians his key to the landscape and its half-hidden resonances; and Bill Gammage, who brought his gift for full imaginative occupation of his subject matter to the all-transforming firestick history of the land.

I said a school, but perhaps that's not quite right. It's more like a camp, a gathering of clear, collaborative voices—and indeed I can picture a campfire of this writing circle, this republic of landscape letters. I can see them in my mind's eye: Tom Griffiths, Mark McKenna, Tim Flannery, Darrell Lewis and many more of them, all close up around the fire and leaning back against their rolled-up swags as the light dies away, and the endless conversation starts—the yarning with no precise aim beyond its own indefinite unfolding and modulation, while the embers spark and the stars wheel on deep into the night. I could single out each of these writers in turn, and write about every one of them with admiration and affection, about them and their golden books—books I have carried with me repeatedly on desert and savannah journeys, and sunk myself into like holy texts.

Each of them has made the landscape and its past

and prospects his chief theme, and woven magic from his involvement with the country and the secrets that it holds, and offers up—but let me take as exemplar just one of their books, a well-known one, the historian Mark McKenna's *Looking for Blackfellas' Point*. I focus on it both for its striking programmatic similarities to *A Million Wild Acres* and its very obvious point of difference. In its pages, McKenna was writing reconciliation literature. His book came out in 2002, and it caught its time. It was a history of the repression of history. It told the story of the settlement of the country just inland from Eden, on the far south coast of New South Wales, where McKenna had implanted himself and was bringing up his young family; but it was also, perforce, the tale of the slow, step-by-step extirpation of the local Aboriginal people from the records, and the blurring of collective memory throughout the southern reaches of the Monaro plateau. After long campaigns and shifts on the hectic stage of national politics, the past was beginning its return, and McKenna's book played its part in this process. Many locals who read it found their ideas about their country changing; some were able to piece together new aspects of the history of their families.

McKenna's aim had been very clear. He, like other conscience-stricken writers of his generation, had wished to repopulate the landscape of Australia's settlement with the Aboriginal people who first held the land and whose presences in it remained so strong that there had been a need to write them out. He brought the Aboriginal peoples of the region back, acting on the idea that this would yield a truer history. Indigenous characters were already present in the work of writers like Rolls, and like Murray, but in McKenna's book they, and their absences, take centre stage, and fill it with a strong surface tone of nostalgia and mourning: a tone that almost masks its wellsprings.

*Looking for Blackfellas' Point* was reissued a decade after its first publication. Of course the political landscape had evolved. The dream of reconciliation with Aboriginal people had been overlaid by a series of new paradigms— intervention, apology, the campaign for constitutional recognition. But Blackfellas' Point itself remained, a soft, curving promontory just up the Towamba River from McKenna's home. He wrote an afterword to the new edition, describing the book's place in his life and thought, and it is an intriguing piece of memoir, a detailed account of 'the one patch of earth to which I most instinctively belong'. The things that have come to matter to him, and the way they matter to him, and the way he expresses their importance to him all remind the reader of the approach taken two decades earlier by his precursors in the tradition.

'I begin,' he writes, 'to understand how crucial my

experience at Blackfellas' Point has been to the development of my writing as a historian. Solitude. Nature. Distance. Space. Independence. All my writing has been completed here. My voice is tied inextricably to the aesthetics of this one place.' The land's look changes, season by season, year by year, but it remains, its presence remains. The natural world invades McKenna's awareness every day:

> A powerful owl slamming up against an upstairs window, its talons spread wide against the frame as it ducks under the eaves to raid a swallow's nest just before dawn; weeds that sprout faster than the time it takes to remove them; drought that grinds down my resilience; king parrots stripping the fruit from our orchard; tiny, insect-eating bats flying into the house through the smallest gap, the persistent beep of their radar emissions keeping me awake at night; a large brown snake trying to force its way inside a flyscreen door; bush rats and antechinus gnawing their way into bedrooms; squadrons of insects attacking my reading lamp every summer evening; wombats bulldozing fences and wallabies eating exotic garden specimens.

No wonder he ends this list with a confession: 'I no longer romanticise nature.' But he has come to know it well, and enter into an intimacy with it: a tie he had longed for, and had obscurely seen as necessary to his writing life. In some profound sense his home country defines him, despite his need to escape its embrace, despite his tending to feel, after long immersion in the landscape, 'as if the valley would swallow me up'. He seeks immersion; he seeks to belong; he feels he does. And yet there is a bend sinister across his heart, which he expresses in his closing words: 'Looking downriver,' he says,

> I've often thought of the tonnes of sand that have buried the riverbed as a metaphor for the concealment of Aboriginal cultural knowledge that occurred in the wake of colonisation. Nearly all the names that were locally bestowed on every plant, creature and landform have been lost, as well as those for the stars in the night sky. Yet my awareness of the magnitude of this cultural loss has not stopped me from belonging to the land. If anything, it has intensified the awe I feel when I contemplate the depth of indigenous knowledge of country. By comparison, my attachment is shallow-rooted and transient.

Inauthentic in his authenticity: a striking thought, coming from so wide-horizon a man—and it reflects the pronounced lean of today's high intelligentsia, for whom

Australia's foundational achievements cannot wash out history's primal stain. This curse is not one that either Eric Rolls or Les Murray, both of them born in the deep bush of New South Wales, felt on their skins when *A Million Wild Acres* came out and received its first critiques, more than three decades ago. In their different ways, each of them had an easy intimacy with the indigenous realm, and with the Aboriginal people they had known all their life in their home surrounds. For them, the landscape was a shared space; it welcomed and it sheltered every living thing.

But when this feeling, this conviction, is no longer predominant, a new settlement with country becomes necessary; it becomes urgent for writers and artists to effect a recalibration—and this is the adjustment that we see being played out in the cultural space in our day. Several pronounced trends in the world of letters reflect this recent shift: the emergence and exaltation of literature by writers of Aboriginal background; the tide of reconciliation-minded historical novels dealing with the epoch of colonial settlement; and the rise of strongly ecological books and essays, works that idealise Australian nature's pristine landscape rather than nature adapted by the incoming hand of western man. In this thought-world, the past era of exclusive indigenous habitation and land use figures as a time when the environment and man were in balance, when an equilibrium and harmony were in place. The type-specimen of this new literary species is a memoir written by the expatriate feminist Germaine Greer, *White Beech: The Rainforest Years*, which has not, in truth, been fully or wholeheartedly absorbed and taken up by the local cultural establishment, perhaps in part because of its arduous prose style, perhaps in part because of the unremittingly harsh verdict it delivers on Australia's history and the devastation visited by incomers upon the land.

Yet *White Beech*, published in 2013, is a true descendant of the tradition begun by *A Million Wild Acres*. It is the tale of a patch of inland forest just north of the border between New South Wales and Queensland, its history, vegetation and wildlife. Above all, it is a love song to a single species, the white beech of the title, *Gmelina leichhardtii*, 'a stupendous tree, growing to forty metres in height, with a straight cylindrical trunk, only slightly flanged at the base'. The book is also the narrative of Greer's decision, in December 2001, to buy herself a patch of rainforest in a locality known as Cave Creek: 'sixty hectares of steep rocky country most of it impenetrable scrub'.

Looking back more than a decade later, Greer describes this shift in her course through the world as 'an extraordinary stroke of luck'. She was settled in her British existence; she lived in tranquil surrounds in rural Essex, writing her occasional books and columns of opinion journalism, performing her sharply delineated role as a public intellectual, maintaining a vexed relationship with the country of her birth. Then she made her visit to the Numinbah Valley, where the Nerang River flows: 'Life grabbed me by the scruff of the neck. I went there as a lamb to the slaughter, without the faintest inkling that my life was about to be taken over by a forest.' As she writes, she found herself there in a realm that was unimaginably vast and ancient. Her horizons flew away; her notions of time expanded and deepened; her self disappeared. She would become the servant of the forest, its advocate, but at the same time just another component element in its connected, interwoven biomass.

She walked down the creek, gazing up at the Bangalow palms and rose apples that soared into the sky, and said to herself, over and over again: Who could own this? 'The azure kingfisher perched on a trembling frond to scan the creek for fish had more right to it than I,' she felt. The eels, scrub-wrens and cicadas were all properly co-owners—and so she christened her land in conformity with the protective venture she was embarking on. It became the Cave Creek Rainforest Rehabilitation Scheme.

For much of its mazy extent, *White Beech* is the chronicle of her efforts to come to terms with the country and piece together the record of its history, both during the colonial settlement of Australia, and in the very different times before Europeans began to farm and fell the eastern coast. The beginnings of the science of rainforest botany, the various schemes put forward to propagate plants from other far-flung possessions of the British empire, Greer's own episodic attempts to make inroads into the Australian desert inland, green tree frogs and their peculiar charms, homestead architecture, bell miners, sea lavender, kangaroo vine and what it tells you—everything is thrown pell-mell into the onrush of the tale, in a manner slightly reminiscent of Eric Rolls at his most staccato.

Greer's personal tics are on full display—her obsessional hatreds, her fondness for piled-up detail, her unending self-involvement. Her strengths, too—the quality she still has of unused-upness; her appetite for knowledge; her active, hectoring presence on the front lines of her life. But it is the intellectual and emotional currents flowing just beneath the surface of *White Beech* that bring it to the eye. Despite the length of her absence from Australia, Greer feels herself tied to the country of her birth. 'Everywhere I had ever travelled across its vast expanse I had seen devastation, denuded hills, eroded slopes, weeds from all over the world, feral animals, open-cut mines as big as cities, salt rivers, salt earth, abandoned townships, whole beaches made of beer cans.' Hence her project—a rehabilitation of land, and a rehabilitation of the landscape-writing tradition.

Half a lifetime after the first appearance of *A Million Wild Acres*, much is changed. The forest landscape of the Pilliga between Baradine and Narrabri is no longer, for all its unemphatic majesty, world enough on its own, nor are the rainforests and the hazy plateaus of the Great Divide. No: consciousness of ourselves and our part in the landscape's story has entered much more into the picture that we see. In his history of place Mark McKenna not only examines the past of the southern Monaro, but seeks to transform it, to rewrite it and reinscribe Aboriginal primacy in the region's records and its archives. The Greer of *White Beech* would prefer to expunge colonial man from the bush forest landscape altogether, the better to restore and preserve the forest's essence and its primal depth. Theirs are both, in their particular ways, projects of moral remediation: literary, historical and practical projects that seek to right a wrong. A great activism has entered into both the stewardship of Australian nature and the rendition of that nature in words.

*

At which juncture, this sequence sketched, let me turn abruptly away, and describe something of my own ideas and intuitions about the country of the far inland, its landscape and its skies; about the sandhill deserts and the tropical savannahs, places where the soils are fine and red, and the eucalypts all burnt, where the spinifex stretches away like a carpet to the horizon line, and mirages shimmer, and kites and eagles patrol the air; about the purple ranges of the Pilbara, and the serrated mountain chains around Lake Argyle; about the sand flats on the shoreline of the Gulf of Carpentaria, and the shaded rivers of Cape York—all these landscapes, and what they hold inside them for me.

But first I should take the story back, back to a quite different view on nature and landscape from the one I have been outlining: the rich tradition that was flourishing in Europe in the early nineteenth century, when Australia was first being opened up to western eyes, the tradition that animates the worldviews of the initial explorers of the inland, Leichhardt especially, and Sturt and Eyre. It is a tradition that worships wilderness, the pure wilderness: wild rivers, deep chasms, the mist of the blue horizon line. This love for untouched nature rhymed uneasily with the mandated economic aims of the great probes and journeys the first explorers made across the Divide, in search of productive country and inland seas or waterways. But its veiled effect may account for their fascination with the seeming emptiness around them, and for something of their reluctance to observe the constant signs they came across of indigenous impact on the land.

It is a worldview that lives above all in literature; it is the sense of the romantic sublime, of the pure heights, where inspiration lurks, and fatal demons, and death as well. It is the romantic spirit one meets in the verse of Shelley and Wordsworth, and in the art of Turner and Caspar David Friedrich; it is in the onrushing literary torrents of Goethe and Rousseau; it gleams in the icy tales of Stifter and Novalis—and its landscape of origin is the high massif of the Alps that lie at the heart of Europe, those peaks of permanent snow, the silent country that pilgrims wishing to reach the Mediterranean and the treasures of the Renaissance were obliged, until the modern era, to traverse on foot, across steep mountain passes bound in ice.

It was in this landscape that I spent much of my childhood—summers, schooldays—in the valleys of the Swiss Engadine: spas and quiet resort towns with green slopes rising up beyond them to the peaks, the bare rock faces and the snowfields reaching up into the sky. I knew the winding paths and the walking trails, and what lay down them—woods and clearings, lakes, views across ravines and river gorges. I can still see the park fountain-springs with their ornate shade cupolas, and the casinos and belvederes, the churches with their towers and their needle spires. I can picture in my mind's eye the shaded path that runs from the village of Sils Maria down the promontory reaching out into the valley lake, and at its end the tall rock with Zarathustra's night song inscribed on its surface: *Oh Mensch,*

*Gieb Acht*—'Man, listen, what speaks in the deep midnight's shade?'

It terrified me then, that carved and transformed rock; I was afraid to go near it, and yet compelled to—and it occurs to me now that such Nietzschean tests in childhood equip one well for whatever might come in the course of life. Those peaks that hemmed in the lake—the Julier, the far Bernina, the Corvatsch—they rose like storm clouds around Sils, where Nietzsche was confined for his life's last decade in his sister's house, unable to speak, unable to pursue the journeys of his thought. He was in the final stage of his derangement; he would howl and howl all through the night. His friend Harry Kessler came to visit, and to bid the philosopher farewell. In a detailed passage of his journal, describing the varied emotions that swept through him during his stay in Sils Maria, Kessler reports that at the goodbye Nietzsche shook his hand, 'peacefully and seriously like a beautiful and loyal animal'.

How strong the contrast was for me in those days between the valleys, choked with all their tradition and history and culture, and the peaks. The peaks were untouched; they were trackless; they were pure. They were the world of beauty, grace and truth: there was nothing human in their vicinity, but they measured man. I remember staring longingly up towards them from the rooms of the

Grand Hotel at Scuol-Tarasp-Vulpera, in the wildest of all the valleys of the Engadine, almost on the borderline between Switzerland and Italy. Every step of that hotel's corridors I can still see today, although it burned down in 1989, and thus has come to symbolise for me the transformation of the divided continent I knew when I was a boy.

For decades after these beginnings I travelled widely, as a correspondent, and I saw many different kinds of landscape—but it was not until I came back to my paternal country, and started revisiting the grey-green bush I used to travel with my father long before, that I felt again, in the far inland, that dissolving fire of clarity and self-loss I felt when I was a child under alpine skies. The join between two fragments of my life had been made—and often it seems to me a join that casts its bridging shadow across everything I seek to write about my experiences and encounters in the deserts and the north. Across the wild bush, too. When I move through that landscape I sense not just its contours and colours, not just its light and shade and its rock formations, but something more, something that seems both within it and beyond it—and even as I seek to capture it, I realise anew that the language we bring to the land is drawn from elsewhere, and is still slowly adapting its words to our surrounds. The bush I find in the remote rangelands is not the enlivened, spirit-laden bush that desert people see in their own country, nor is it that landscape covered over by the past, and full of names and recorded memories, that we confront in western countries where vanished time hangs in the air like an all-shading veil of damp, heart-chilling cloud. Whether in the back country of the De Grey River or the mulga plains of western Queensland, the sense I have in silent moments is similar. I feel a distance. I feel something remote, yet watchful: a distant presence.

At the outset, when I was beginning these private little sorties and journeys of discovery of mine into the inland, years ago, I had no reasoned or well-developed idea of why it was I might want to give such attention to the country, rather than merely observe it and traverse it—and I went about my task, my program, methodically, but without great thought. Things only crystallised for me in more recent times, when I came across a long recorded interview with Alexander Solzhenitsyn, the writer I admire more than any other of our age, for the artistry of his magnum opus, *The Gulag Archipelago*, as much as for its strength of witness. Its greatness is plainer still now its immediate time is gone; it is universal, not specific, and its granite strength seems linked to the peculiar circumstances of its composition: Solzhenitsyn was free, but under sharp surveillance, harried, troubled, forever moving, forced to write his words on stray leaves of paper, never in possession of a unitary manuscript. It was made in fragments but the work itself has no fissures, no imperfections.

The filmed exchanges between Solzhenitsyn and the documentarist Alexander Sokurov run for more than three hours; the talk swirls here and there, but there is one moment that made a great impact on me. The film-maker takes the writer's hands and holds them. The words stop. The soundtrack is just Solzhenitsyn's breathing—for a minute, two. Breath, life. It is the simplest, most intimate scene I have come across in this genre.

The two men discuss the place of nature in the world of art. Solzhenitsyn had a clear view, unsurprisingly, having spent so much of his life plunged amid nature: involuntarily, when he was jailed in Gulag camps in the deeps of the Siberian taiga; by choice, when he was expelled from his own country and took refuge in the United States, in the state of Vermont, surrounded by its forests of maple and pine and spruce and yellow birch. There is a beauty in nature, Solzhenitsyn believes, and it has a purpose, or a consequence. 'Beauty is the light of truth seen through matter,' he says. 'It ennobles.' It lifts us up; it reveals the order of the world, and of ourselves. But there is apocalypse ahead, he says, a few words later, speaking simply, in a matter-of-fact voice: nature is dying. 'We are going to destroy nature. It is dying inexorably.'

As I was drawing these ideas about landscape and landscape writing in Australia into focus in my thoughts, I had to make a trip north from the Queensland coastal wet tropics, through the savannah country, up the central spine of Cape York; and the initial stages of the journey were enough to bring that judgement of Solzhenitsyn's back to me, as indeed, are most long drives that set out from the settled coastal country and head through the zone of agricultural exploitation into the more inhospitable reaches of the hot, arid bush.

The first stretch of that road, the Mulligan Highway, is heavily travelled in the cool times of the year, by mining supply trucks and by the unending-seeming procession of four-wheel-drive caravaners who want to tick off the long straight track to the tip of Cape York. About half an hour beyond the Palmer River roadhouse, an old structure built from sombre bluestone, there is a turn-off. This is the Peninsula Development Road, which traverses the Lakeland subdivision, a farming area, named not for its landscape— although it has a network of agricultural infrastructure and dams and irrigation systems—but for the early gold prospector William Lakeland, who passed through the area, well armed, in the 1870s.

Lakeland is a recent creation, but it is already a palimpsest-like landscape, filled with the remains of unprofitable ventures once supported and promoted by the state. Decaying teak trees and peanut groves dot the area. Amid dead plants, a new banana plantation lines the northeast side of the road for several kilometres. There are modern packing sheds, and dormitory accommodation blocks for seasonal workers. Along the frontage of the tamed and channelled river there are farm homesteads, many of them prefabricated steel-span structures, the new quick-start lodging of the north. None of this has anything to do with the tropical savannah, which resumes abruptly once the land begins to rise up from the plain: anthills, gumtrees; the sequence of cattle stations begins afresh. The high sandstone ranges, rich in Quinkan rock art, enclose the road. Laura community looms up. It is the whole story, without a gear change: the measured realm of nature, the hectic world of man. Only one speaks to us. What is the secret it seems to whisper? What do we hear there? What does it know that lies in wait along our road ahead? It completes us; it is the screen against which we can sense and see ourselves.

Increasingly I feel the horizon in its silence is given to us as a clue; that time is the cocooning, nurturing chrysalis that holds us, within which we must come to understand our being and seek to perfect ourselves; and that the landscape, the natural world, the unending bush is the veil around us through which we must see. What we cannot know is the marker line that leads us on; what is unwritten in nature is what most frees us. We are change, and thought, and death: it in all its rhythms is changelessness.

# VI

# The Gleam of the Outsider

*Seeing with Wide Eyes*

When I was a boy I attended an international school on the shores of Lake Geneva, near Lausanne, a city with few distractions to offer its visitors: but a new kind of art museum had recently opened there, and it was filled with striking objects—sculptures made from shells or from tide-worn driftwood, intensely detailed paintings of clouds and atmospheric phenomena, abstractions that had the feel of fever dreams. This was the Collection de l'Art Brut, an assemblage of 'outsider' works gathered up by the French painter Jean Dubuffet over the course of several decades. And that initial, youthful encounter of mine with outsider art, then still little known and scarcely recognised as a legitimate current of creative endeavour, brings many thoughts to mind today, in a very different time—an era when almost every member of the contemporary art elite wishes to be seen as a rebel, an outsider, an outlaw, far removed from the staid thought-worlds of convention and privilege.

What can the tale of Art Brut and its reception tell us? Can it serve us as a secret mirror of ourselves, or reflect our fond hopes for knowledge of the sensuous world around us, and the veiled layers of the cosmos that seem to rest beyond our easy reach? What can the outsiders bring to us, or we to them? Rather than seeking to provide some sweeping, all-defining set of answers to these questions, my aim is to edge towards them, to move into their foothills, and look up towards their heights—and present a handful of my own impressions and experiences of this artistic current over the years, as my eyes and my sense of what surrounds us and awaits us have evolved—and I must begin in Lausanne, on the shores of the lake, the lake that has given peace and shelter to a long line of non-conformists: to Voltaire, to Rousseau, to Nabokov, and in our time to the pioneering impresario of outsider art as well.

Dubuffet, the great codifier of this tradition, was, at the apogee of his renown some two generations ago, a cultural celebrity of the first rank—a circumstance that pained him greatly, as did his personal background. His father was a prosperous wine merchant, from the port town of Le Havre in Normandy, and Dubuffet himself, after a brief spell of formal art studies at the Académie Julian, went into the family business. Wartime came, and the years of German military occupation: he made large profits from his dealings with the Wehrmacht. But he also liked to move in literary circles; he had a taste for writers on the edge of things. He knew Michaux, Paulhan, Ponge and Artaud, and painted their portraits in a flat, austere, somewhat confrontational style. Soon enough he drew close to the surrealists. He even gave financial support to that walker down dark byways Louis-Ferdinand Céline.

Given such associations and such leanings, it was no surprise that a strong streak of hostility to the art establishment increasingly took hold of Dubuffet and came to dominate his thinking. His theoretical texts, which he poured out in great profusion, are replete with idealising praise of tribal cultures and primitivism. He loved all artwork that seemed untutored, freely made, devoid of the marks of technique or professional skill. By the early 1960s he had embedded himself in the front line of the European avant-garde.

He began making his colossal polystyrene sculptures, to which he gave the nonsense name L'Hourloupe. Their contours and their facets were daubed in vinyl acrylic—red, black and a rich blue. The design pattern, repeated constantly with minor variations, had come to him while he was doodling on a pad of paper during a long telephone call; he felt that these L'Hourloupe lines had revealed to him the way images surface and come to life in the ferment of the mind. Soon he was building L'Hourloupe figure groups, L'Hourloupe towers and monoliths, entire buildings of jagged, roughly stencilled polystyrene, L'Hourloupe precincts to serve as meditative spaces and escapes from the press of contemporary life. Their success was immediate, and overwhelming: during the mid-1960s they were everywhere in the great modern-art collections and high-end galleries of the West.

Dubuffet, though, saw himself increasingly as an outsider, and wished to be seen as one. He believed in low art, distrusted good taste, and loathed the classical canon. He began to track down the works of pure invention that appealed to him. He discovered outsiders, he nurtured them, he collected their art in quantity: the cork carvings of the Catalan Joaquim Vicens Gironella; the passion images of Aloïse Corbaz, who made her works with the juice from petals, from crushed leaves and toothpaste; the halo forms of the asylum patient Adolf Wölfli; the mediumistic abstracts of Laure Pigeon. Dubuffet's own fame has almost evaporated now, but he would be overjoyed by this eclipse, and by the rise in reputation of the Art Brut treasures that were the centre of his collecting life—the jewels he amassed with such studious attention and such committed care.

*

Even in the very first days of his foundation, it had the air of a temple sacred to strange, unreachable gods. The pieces were displayed in a purpose-built set of galleries through which one wandered as if in a maze, without signs to orient one. There was nothing at all to indicate the provenance of the various artworks, nothing to situate them in the history of cultures or the flow of time. In that collection, which I came to know during the same years that I first saw and became familiar with the more canonical museums and galleries of Western Europe, everything seemed turned upside down. I had never seen the like of those objects before; they were made by men and women whose names I had never heard spoken. The paintings and drawings failed to confront or meet the eye. They kept to themselves; they made no invitation for one to join them in a world of shared, familiar associations. The carved pieces were not figures, so much as impressions—feelings given direct form. In that villa in the back streets of Lausanne's Beaulieu district, art was telling broken stories; it was slipping the accepted bonds of narrative. It was exorbitant; it was disturbing the peace rather than keeping it.

Only now, as I look back from half a lifetime on, do I come to see how much the Art Brut collection shaped and influenced me, how much its works opened my thoughts to the idea that beauty is not by definition serene or calm, that meaning is not always to be fully or successfully translated or decoded, that symbols gain from a degree of elusiveness. As I explored my way through those galleries on weekend afternoons, I came almost to suspect that civilisation is held in place as much by the structures on its outmost margins as by its tightly clustered central columns—those shining temple columns with their carved words of law. Dreams without words filled me when I was there: I knew I was beyond the borders of the world I was being schooled for and prepared to enter. I told myself that art could be the highway between the forces in the world around us and the receptive mind of man.

But these intuitions took form in me only gradually; they were not well-developed notions, passed down in texts or schoolbooks; they had no link to the realm of logic; and as I try now to trace their origins I feel sure they were in some sense effects of the landscapes I found myself surrounded by in those years of boyhood—dramatic landscapes: the alpine peaks one could see rising beyond the far shore of the still lake on summer days, or the birch forests and green, silent river valleys of southern Bohemia, or the snow-clad mountain passes of the Engadine.

What did these wild places have in common with the works on view in the Art Brut collection? One thing: they were free from western culture's controlling stamp, its great, coherent, overarching belief system, enshrined and codified in imagery. The peaks of the Alps rose far beyond the reach of roads and tracks, beyond the world of landscapes husbanded by man; and the Lausanne paintings and carved and sculpted pieces were free from all the precepts of artistic composition. Their makers did not know the rules of colour harmony, and perspective; they were not stalked and shadowed by the achievements of the Renaissance or the modes of modernism.

In his passionate collecting and his long journeyings through the archipelago of outsider creativity, Dubuffet was strongly influenced by the first exploration of the genre, *Bildnerei der Geisteskranken*, a majestic monograph written in 1922 by the Heidelberg psychiatrist Hans Prinzhorn, a man fascinated by the borderlands between inspired artistry and full-blown mental illness. Prinzhorn had served as an army surgeon in the Great War. He used art-making in his therapeutic endeavours; he saw the parallels between visionary illness and prophetic insight. These ideas guided him in his selection of the works he singled out for close attention, and they also, decades later, guided Dubuffet, many of whose earliest Art Brut pieces were drawn from the leading mental asylums and sanatoria of the continent. Here he is, very much in Prinzhorn's footsteps, describing the field in an essay written for a show he organised in Paris, in 1949:

By this, by Art Brut, we mean pieces of work executed by people untouched by artistic culture, in which therefore mimicry, contrary to what happens in intellectuals, plays little or no part, so that their authors draw everything from their own depths and not from clichés of classical art or art that is fashionable. Here we are witnessing an artistic operation that is completely pure, raw, reinvented in all its phases by its author, based solely on his own impulses. Art, therefore, in which is manifested the sole function of invention, and not those, constantly seen in cultural art, of the chameleon and the monkey.

Dropouts, deviators, refusers, autists—terms of this kind recur in the early Art Brut critical literature. The Lausanne scholar Michel Thévoz, Dubuffet's collaborator and successor, is more explicit. It is his view that Art Brut allows its creators to escape from the field of cultural attraction and from mental norms: 'And certainly it is of madness that we need to speak, even if the term is exempted from its pathological connotations. The creative process is triggered off as unpredictably as a psychotic episode, articulating itself according to its own logic, like an invented language.'

Such were the principles that led Dubuffet on as he amassed his collection of gemlike works by unknown art-makers: masters who built up their own enclosed worlds in their works—works quite free from the tropes one finds in the academy or in the avant-garde.

*

How, though, to frame them? How to draw close to them? The arguments advanced by Dubuffet and taken up by the growing coterie of scholars and collectors and enthusiasts of outsider art tend to highlight the uniqueness of the style. It is a tradition, but a tradition of soloists. It is the mind set free from the chains of convention, but caught within its own chains. It reaches for the sublime; it dwells in the stars. It is compulsive art, not an art that comes to our eyes filtered or modulated or refined. As such, it is routinely presented as something uniquely precious—integral, primal, dusted with a kind of sacred innocence: the one current, in a world of falseness and surface shimmer, that can be seen as unalloyed and true.

This familiar case for outsider creativity has been current since the cultural upheavals of the 1960s, but it marks a departure from the initial impulse that drove researchers and psychiatric practitioners to examine and analyse the works their patients made. The first hope was that the art produced in the locked wards of asylums might facilitate diagnosis, might shed light on the workings of an obscure internal world, might even hold out some promise of therapeutic benefits. It was a means to alleviate suffering—nothing more. Indeed, it is only in our time that outsider art has come to occupy its exalted position in the firmament of contemporary culture. Derangement has become a high card: van Gogh's example tells the tale. Mental turmoil is seen as cousin to insight, and to a privileged understanding of man's place in the world.

This shift has been made possible only by a turn of our attention away from the experience of the makers of outsider art, to the impact their work makes upon its viewers, connoisseurs of the contemporary, watchers of the cultural menagerie, alert to anything that might be new and unconstrained. And this, of course, is the realisation of Dubuffet's worst nightmare: the ziggurat of high art is claiming suzerainty over the last free spirits still aloft on the wings of pure creation, still spontaneous—still beyond its all-corroding reach.

\*

Some years later, at the time in life when the mind begins to open, I struck out on my own, and started making journeys out into the surrounding landscape, which I had known until then only as a playground, all forest paths and mountain tracks. I travelled to new towns; I crossed borders; I made a trip to Basel, and saw its grandiose cathedral, the stage-set for Carl Jung's famous dream in which he grasped for the first time the scale of God's absence from the world of man. I found my way to the art museum, which still bore the strong imprint of the city's humanist scholars. Its prime exhibit, in those days, shown in a white cube-like room, was the depiction of the dead Christ after the deposition from the cross, by Hans Holbein the Younger. Christ's body in the tomb: a sombre work. God's son, mortal, made of weak, pale, livid flesh.

As it happens, this same painting made a deep impression on Dostoyevsky when he made his visit to Western Europe with his young wife, Anna Grigoryevna, in 1867. The couple arrived in Switzerland in early August. They spent a day in Basel, much of it in the museum. Their guide steered them towards the Holbein: 'As a rule,' wrote Anna that night in her diary, 'one sees Jesus Christ painted after his death with his face all tortured and suffering, but his body with no marks on it at all of pain and suffering—though of course they must have been there.' How broken the form of Christ on the canvas had seemed to her—life-sized, pierced with wounds, swollen, the skin on the point of decomposition. She was reluctant to linger before the image. Her husband, though, was 'completely carried away by it, and in his desire to look at it closer got on a chair, so that I was in a terrible state lest he should have to pay a fine, as one is always liable to here'.

In her later reminiscences, Anna gives further detail: she came back some minutes later to find Dostoyevsky still staring at the work, riveted to the same spot. 'His agitated face had a kind of dread in it, something I had noticed more than once during the first moments of an epileptic seizure.' When Dostoyevsky came to write *The Idiot*, his tale of a naïve and Christ-like hero, the Holbein painting figures prominently. His central character, Prince Myshkin, comes upon a reproduction of the work in the house of his great rival. It fills Myshkin with holy dread, and seems to intensify his faith. But one character, the pure, consumptive Ippolit Terentyev, finds in the painting only a challenge to all belief:

> It conjures up an image of nature as death, nature in the form of a huge machine of the most modern construction, which, dull and insensible, has clutched, crushed and swallowed up a great priceless Being, a Being worth all nature and its laws, worth the whole earth, which was perhaps created solely for the appearance of that Being.

A telling transformation has taken place. The divine deranges. Faith's image brings the writer to the point of mental seizure; belief wavers, beauty fails in its task of reflecting the grace of life.

I too remember with great exactitude my first impression

of this painting. It reminded me of the more tormented Art Brut works I knew from Lausanne, which had until then been my chief measure of ecstatic insight. It filled me with troubled thoughts. Art of this kind spoke to me then not of its maker's mastery and skill, but of mortal fears, and servitude; the world it made palpable was one of pain, and obligation; the horizon it conceived beyond us was a dark vanishing point. It offered up a still screen of suffering, a dictatorial meditation space with no way out. How entangled it seemed in past tales and traditions it was condemned to recount endlessly: how trapped, how caught.

The decades since have stilled those impressions in me, and papered them over—but not entirely done away with them. What higher realm does religious art purport to show? What special quality distinguishes its accepted masterpieces, the totemic objects of our long-preserved western culture? What sets them apart? When I hold the jewels of the Dubuffet collection in balance in my thoughts against the galleries full of Italian and Flemish Madonnas that fill the museums of Europe, it seems plain that there is little to choose between them in terms of purely visual wonder, the delight they bring the eye. The obvious distinction is in technique, in the regularity of the composition—but the deeper difference lies in the legibility of the two schools, the ways in which we comprehend them.

Outsider art, although it very often seeks after and records spiritual insight, remains beyond our ken. We may find its works lovely, and compelling, but we cannot place them or fix them neatly in the order of our thoughts. Religious art of similar pitch and intent slips easily into our hearts and minds because we have been prepared for it. Those figures and their attitudes, their smooth harmonies of colour, their messages of transcendence—we know them well; they are part of our common vocabulary of images and forms. And this is the easy, tempting schema for considering the art of outsiders, the art of those Prinzhorn categorised almost a century ago as unstable, insane, sick in the soul. Established art as the royal road to truth and harmony; outsider works as effusions from the human spirit's pale, ill-charted frontier lands.

Behind this schema lurks a last, unacknowledged architecture that shapes us all: our thoughts, our language, the great ordered cathedrals of our selves. Our minds are schooled by words, by ideas expressed through words, by the image systems we share through our common culture. All these forces serve as disciplines, as filters, allowing us to know and name and negotiate the world about us, and to maintain an internal conversation with ourselves. It is at the points of imperfection in this system of insulations and protections that our sense of the uncanny enters in: at such points that intimations of a further presence in our thought-world make their claims. Since time immemorial we have built religions to absorb these moments, moments when pure sensation flashes through us. We have built a set of concepts to give the flaws in our world map a meaning and a sense.

For those we now describe as outsiders, though, things seem to go differently, and I tend to feel in many cases that this is because the languages and beliefs we use in common have less of a hold on them. The fit between world and mind is different; there are different paths between the two realms laid down. And perhaps something of this way of seeing the divide between the outsider category and the more settled lowlands of creativity was already half-formed in my thoughts a few years later, when the first canonic presentation of Art Brut's masterpieces in a western capital city went on view. This was the *Outsiders* exhibition, mounted almost a generation ago at the Hayward Gallery on London's South Bank: it took on the historic significance it now holds only in retrospect. There was nothing accidental about the staging of a similar survey show in the same institution, with much greater fanfare, in 2013. The opening night of that more recent exhibition, attended as it was by the flower of the continent's intelligentsia, nicely illustrates the advance of the outsider genre from the margins of the art establishment to a more respectable niche in the theme park of contemporary cultural forms.

I was a young student at the time of the first Hayward show; I was living in France, and very much under the influence of the philologist André Walther. He was a revolutionary socialist, and a veteran of the uprising in Lisbon, the Carnation Revolution that had overthrown the dictatorship of Salazar, an event he recalled often, in the most fervent terms. We took the night train across the Channel, and arrived at the Hayward early on the first morning of the show—and although I find it almost incredible to relate this, we had with us a large professional camera, and, instead of a tripod, an ironing board as its support, and we were allowed in to the galleries and wandered through them with this equipment in tow. Every so often, André would stop and set up the ironing board, place his camera on it, focus with great care and take close-up images of works that particularly struck him. His verdict was unfavourable.

'It's just more superstitious claptrap,' he said. 'It's the voice of the past.'

I, by contrast, was greatly moved by a range of the exhibits. I already knew the work of several of the artists being shown: Madge Gill, Nek Chand, Clément Fraisse. There was an ink sketch on paper by Laure Pigeon in the most haunting blues and blacks: nets, veils, elusive shadings and lines. There were scrawled message-texts from asylum inmates to the lost or imagined objects of their love and longing. There were hallucinatory visions of divine armies in the heavens; there were sculpted faces cut from ground and coloured glass; there were solemn, cryptic masks made up of shells.

'I always feel as if I'm almost in a new creation when I see this kind of art,' I said to André.

'Nonsense,' he replied. 'You just don't understand the power of the prevailing system to recuperate everything— everything flows into its order. Even madness. Even works made in institutions cut off from the exchange networks we live with. All this is consumerist fantasy: the trap of desire, the same everywhere. There's no rationale for dividing art-makers into the categories of respectable and insane.'

'Are you trying to tell me,' I asked him, 'that there's no physical basis for the conditions we treat as mental illness?'

'That's an interesting question,' he began, and then suddenly fell silent.

We had reached a side gallery hung with brightly coloured, cartoon-like works. They were by Henry Darger, who was completely unknown at that time, though in the years since he has become the most famous and most admired of all the outsider artists of the century just past. We stood and gazed. Before our eyes was a landscape, pink skies, blue hills, a crowded scene of figures, girls with fringe-cut hair, in various states of undress, running, hiding, their movements strangely in lockstep.

'Just look at those colours,' said André. 'What combinations! I've never seen anything so lovely.' He laughed. 'Maybe there is something in this outsider story after all.'

Strange tales circulated about Darger back then: he had seen his entire family wiped out by a volcanic eruption in his native Mexico; he was descended from Hapsburg royalty; he was a religious mystic and obsessive collector of street rubbish from the neighbourhoods around his home on Chicago's North Side. The truth was at once more sublunary and more remarkable: he was incarcerated for some years in an asylum, then released; he supported himself by working as a hospital porter, and in his tiny apartment he poured out the tens of thousands of pages of manuscript and traced out the illustrations that constitute his artwork. How to receive the gifts such paintings and drawings give? How to understand them, and place them?

*

A short while after that trip to the Hayward I left academic philology behind, and spiralled off into a reporting career; and as I look back on my life's episodes now, I see that I was drawn insistently to remote cultures and their traditions: Mayan, Anatolian, Melanesian, Ambonese. It was not until I came back to my father's country after a long apprenticeship in foreign corresponding that I found a stable foothold, and felt that I could bring together and turn over all the sights that I had seen. I soon embarked on a series of extended assignments in the north of Australia, and in the centre, and in the course of those journeys, naturally enough, I encountered Aboriginal art, which was then enjoying its initial vogue. Collectors, curators and carpetbaggers were out in the field. It was easy enough to pick up the basics of the trade in indigenous art, and the widely shared assumptions and preconceptions that had sprung up to place and frame the works these experts promoted and bought and sold.

The Australian indigenous artist was seen, somehow, as distinct: separated from the western art-lover by a profound, unbridgeable divide. The art-maker from the Aboriginal remote-community domain was not merely an individual, but also the bearer of a tradition, the Dreaming. The imprint of this tradition was in the mind of the artist, in the blood. Paintings and carved objects held value to the degree that they carried the Dreaming's essence within them. If they seemed beautiful, it was because this mystic force was present in their patterns, their arcs and dots and lines. One might try to comprehend such works by learning something of the Aboriginal mythologies and story cycles from the artist's particular region, but the secret core of the Dreaming would remain forever out of reach: indeed, it was the distanced, unknowable quality of the art's inner meaning that lay at the heart of its appeal. It was decorative, it was composed in pleasing colours, but these elements of the painting tradition were merely the surface trappings. This was art as impenetrable screen, as icon image. The most hieratic works were conceived precisely to mask and shroud the after-echoes of divine creation in the Dreamtime, far off yet ever present, when the tradition's immutable laws and precepts were first laid down.

When the distinctive features of the indigenous art tradition—and its purest and best-known exemplar, the Western Desert painting movement—are sketched out in this way, the parallels with outsider work become quite clear. Both art currents have flourished over the same period of mounting anomie in mainstream western culture; both appeal to the same kinds of enthusiasts; both depend for their pull on the same sense of irremediable distance between the art-maker and the admirer of the work. Yet the actual positions and roles of the two groups of art-makers in their respective worlds are vastly different. Many outsiders still operate very much on the margins of the contemporary social and cultural landscape, while indigenous artists in Australia are greatly respected, if from a certain distance. Outsiders may be confined, or live in care or under medication, in a bid to treat the symptoms of their conditions; but in the remote indigenous realm, visions and experiences of psychic transport are viewed as proofs of spiritual insight and seniority in Law.

Prophetic dreams and paranormal experiences are not only frequent but are seen as veridical, as the core material of existence, as the key to daily life.

How, given all this, not to reflect that the chief similarity between the outsider and the indigenous remote-community traditions is the psychic work both do in our minds? But how not to wonder, in the same thought, whether there might be a human spectrum, along which artists can be ranged according to the links between those wordless intuitions that come to them and the worldly ordering that guides and channels the responses of their minds? A striking notion.

Yet it is equally striking how little attention has been paid until now by the critical establishment to the close parallels between the reception of outsider art and Aboriginal art. It was not until the exhibition of a series of remarkable artworks, in mid-2013, in—of all places—tranquil, tropical Cairns that these similarities began to come into focus.

*Renegades* was a shoestring show put on at an obscure venue, KickArts Contemporary, in central Abbott Street. It brought together a diverse selection of non-mainstream artists, and hung their works close together in a promiscuous manner. It was an exhibition that sought out visual rhymes rather than social affinities. It displayed works by outsiders, by the self-taught and by art-makers on the far geographic fringes of the continent—works far removed from the world of taste and mode and fashion: indeed, it seemed inclusive to such a degree it almost abjured the idea of formal program or concerted exhibition plan. But *Renegades* was one of those freewheeling art events that somehow express a higher truth. There were ceramic sculptures, embroidered tableaux, fetish figures made from papier-mâché; there were works by studio-based western outsiders, by the reclusive and the self-dependent, by indigenous men and women on disability programs, and by senior artists from the furthest corners of the Torres Strait. I saw the exhibition pieces first in the KickArts storerooms, in bad lighting, piled here and there. This lent them a further inexplicable charm. I remember the impact those objects made on me: the striated, twisted walking sticks carved by Peter Drewitt, the painstaking watercolours of Kapua Gutchen from remote Darnley Island, the scale-model light plane depicting left and right freedoms by Bernard Vartuli, the wild black brumby portrait by the Pitjantjatjara artist Lance James.

What thoughts *Renegades* set into flight—links and parallels that seemed to point the way towards a more synoptic apprehension of the art we see and the world that art reflects.

Some months after the close of the exhibition at KickArts, it became essential for me to make a visit, for research purposes of my own, to the university town of Heidelberg, a place I had always avoided, because of its dark historical associations and because of the natural fear such hallowed destinations evoke in one of disappointment when the imagination's view is replaced by the more fitful and incoherent experiences that come from life itself. I had the picture of the castle and its majestic gardens and the philosophers' walk well established in my mind. I could see Brentano and Achim von Arnim in those courtyards, strolling, conversing, gazing out across the river.

I was keen to follow in their steps—but as I was on my way towards the old quarter, just, in fact, as I was passing the great hall of the university, where so many words of leaden import for our culture have been spoken, my eye was caught by a discreet little sign. SAMMLUNG PRINZHORN, it read. I diverted, and made my way through a warren of small, well-kept faculty buildings, through automatically opening glass sliding doorways, down corridors, until I reached a silent, deserted, well-kept museum. One entered by going down a flight of stairs, as if into a burial chamber. Faint light beams fell from the ceiling upon a handful of objects—scraps of paper, sketches, rough-carved figurines. A brief note recorded the life and achievements of Prinzhorn, whose career and character had been a blur to me, though I had scanned through the pages of his *Artistry of the Mentally Ill* repeatedly, and I went back to it in the months that followed, and steeped myself in its depths.

Prinzhorn's first aim was to establish the field of outsider creativity: by showing the work of asylum patients to reveal their gifts, their profound way with intuition expressed as design. He had no interest in presuming to interpret the work of outsiders, or claiming in any way to unravel the turmoil of the mind. It seems plain that he was somewhat trapped by academic language and by the logic of systems, and it is almost as if the majestic images he included in his book were his sole means of breaking free. There is beauty in the world of the outsiders, he argues: who are we to judge the merits of their work? Were the images the patients made not eruptions of a universal creative urge—flare signals sent up to combat the dreadful isolation imposed by illness of the mind? Here he is, making the claim:

> If we have to define the crucial criterion of our observational method more precisely, we remind the reader of Count Tolstoy's concept of art—to assume a basic, universal human process behind the aesthetic and cultural surface of the configurative process would be entirely consistent with it. That basic process would be essentially the same in the most sovereign drawing by Rembrandt as in the most miserable daubing by a paralytic: both would be expressions of the psyche.

This revolutionary doctrine matched the spirit of the times. It took hold, and briefly swept Prinzhorn's work to prominence, and the collection he had helped establish to something approaching fame. The similarities between the artworks of clinic patients and the German avant-garde were evident to all who read his richly illustrated study on its first publication soon after the Great War's end. The further fearful analogy he wished to draw was also clear. Just as Prinzhorn could point to 'a link between the schizophrenic outlook of mental patients and the style of the expressionists', so he saw collapse and breakdown in the world structures of the time.

> The schizophrenic artist has to adapt to the fateful psychotic alienation and transformation of his world, while the mentally healthy artist turns away consciously from the familiar reality, from the compulsion of external appearances, in order to meet the decay of the formerly predominant outlook with the autonomous self.

A mad age needed a mad art to match and mirror its own surrounds.

Prinzhorn's own fate seems bound up with his outlook. He had too many gifts: he was a scholar, and a creative spirit, and a seeker after the deep structures of the world. His restlessness was palpable. He had degrees in art history and philosophy from Vienna; he translated Gide and D. H. Lawrence; he was a trained lyric baritone. He turned to medicine only in his late twenties. It was a surrender to his sense of mankind's suffering, adrift in modernity.

Some years after his foundational researches in Heidelberg, he went on a lecture tour of the United States, and we have a record of a social evening he spent at the home of a faculty colleague in Yellow Springs, Ohio. His hostess happened to find Prinzhorn leafing through an album of Schubert songs on the piano: he was asked to sing, and gave an impromptu performance of these incomparably mournful works. The psychoanalyst David Watson, who later wrote an appreciation of Prinzhorn, *In the Teeth of All Formalism*, was present that night, and he recalls how he was 'reduced to tears by the magnificence of the artistic experience'.

Prinzhorn travelled on from the Midwest. He made for the remote upland reaches of the Mexican cordillera to study the use by traditional tribal Indians of narcotic drugs. Soon afterwards, a victim of typhus contracted in southern Italy, he died in Munich, aged only forty-seven. A handful of the paintings and sketches he had gathered up for the collection in Heidelberg were put on view in the special exhibition of Degenerate Art the National Socialist regime mounted in its glory years. The rest were packed away in the attics of the university's school of art.

Such was the man who pioneered the field of outsider creation, who first classified its works, and who bowed his head in admiration before the beauties and the mysteries he found in asylum wards. He was, of course, an outsider himself—a figure transfixed by the longing to see beyond the semblances our life, and glimpse the shining, pulsing centre of our world.